Bicycling Magazine's

Bicycle Commuting Made Easy

Bicycling Magazine's
Bicycle Commuting Made Easy

By the Editors of *Bicycling* Magazine

Rodale Press, Emmaus, Pennsylvania

Compiled by *Ed Pavelka*

Edited by *Kathleen A. Becker*

Production editor: *Jane Sherman*

Copy editor: *Durrae Johanek*

Cover and interior design: *Lisa Farkas*

Book layout: *Peter A. Chiarelli*

Cover photo: *Nathan Bilow*

If you have any questions or comments concerning this book, please write:
    Rodale Press
    Book Reader Service
    33 East Minor Street
    Emmaus, PA 18098

Library of Congress Cataloging-in-Publication Data

Bicycling magazine's bicycle commuting made easy / by the editors of
    Bicycling magazine.
        p.   cm.
    Includes bibliographical references.
    ISBN 0–87596–101–0 paperback
    1. Bicycle commuting.   I. Bicycling.   II. Title: Bicycle
commuting made easy.
    HE6736.B53   1992
    629.28′472—dc20   91–45292
                                                                 CIP

Distributed in the book trade by St. Martin's Press

2 4 6 8 10 9 7 5 3 1 paperback

CONTENTS

◼️ INTRODUCTION

You're reading this because you're at a crossroads. You're thinking about doing something that will save money, improve your health, and protect the environment. You're thinking about becoming a bicycle commuter. You know it's the right thing to do, but you're not sure how—or even if it's possible in your personal situation.

Let me assure you of three things: Bike commuting is easy, it's enjoyable, and anyone can fit it into his or her life. I know because it has become part of mine. I've learned the truth in the statement, "The only valid reason not to commute by bike is that you don't want to." This was said by John Kukoda, a senior editor at *Bicycling* magazine who has been cycling 10 miles to work and back for more than six years. (And if you think John is wrong, that you may have some unconquerable obstacles, he will lay them to rest in chapter 2.)

This is your handbook for bike commuting. In these pages you'll find expert tips from real commuters on everything from riding confidently in traffic to simplified bike maintenance. There are answers to your questions about clothing, accessories, choosing or modifying a bike, and riding in darkness or poor weather. You'll also find up-to-date information about the effects of commuting on your health and diet.

It's been said that the hardest thing about bike commuting is taking the first ride. Once you begin, it will soon become a positive part of your life. And that's what makes it so easy.

Ed Pavelka, Editor-at-Large
Bicycling Magazine

Part One
GETTING STARTED

1 AN EDITOR BECOMES A COMMUTER

If 77 million U.S. adults ride a bike at least occasionally, how come only 2.6 million use one for daily transportation? It's a perplexing question considering the personal, economic, and environmental benefits of cycling.

Why, even Ed Pavelka an editor at *Bicycling* magazine, is not immune to procrastinating about bike commuting. A cyclist since 1972, Ed raced and trained year-round for fitness but never rode to work or for errands. Then one day in 1990 he finally decided to park his car and give commuting a try for 30 days. What follows are the highlights of his experience, which will help you understand what it takes to begin commuting and how expectations compare to reality.

From a Meeting to the Road

Monday, October 15. It's 7:00 A.M. and I'm sitting in managing editor Joe Kita's office, realizing we're hypocrites. We've been thinking aloud about how more people seem to be considering riding a bike to work or school. The question is: How can *Bicycling* help them?

Well, how the heck would we know? We don't commute by bike. I ride an average of 9,600 miles a year, but nary a one in place of driving a car. Instead, my 25-mile daily round trip to work takes place in a Plymouth Voyager. It's the same for Joe, who lives a bit farther away but also has a pleasant rural route.

3

In fact, most staffers have no good excuse, but only two are committed bike commuters. A few others do it occasionally, when the weather is nice.

So I hit Joe with this idea: "How about if one of the editors rides a bike to work every day for a month, no matter what, and writes an article about it? You know—the good, the bad, and the ugly. What it requires in everything from equipment to lifestyle changes. This would show readers what it would be like if they did it. Whaddaya think?"

"Great idea," says Joe. "Who you gonna make do it."

Pause. Gulp. "Me."

"Ha! When?"

"I'll start November 1."

Taking the First Steps

Thursday, November 1. I'm driving to work and feeling extra hypocritical. My ability to procrastinate on commuting might be worthy of a listing in *Guinness.* In fact, the reason I volunteered is because I've toyed with the idea of bike commuting for several years but never had the impetus to start. In the end, I rejected it for the same reasons that might be stopping you: Commuting will take the fun out of cycling, it isn't sufficient training, it takes too much time, it's dangerous to ride in darkness and bad weather, it requires buying special equipment, it's a hassle to carry home-work and office clothes, clean up . . . and on and on.

Enough! I'm starting today to get the necessary equipment together. The new target date is November 15. Yeah, this is the threshold of winter weather and minimal daylight here in Pennsylvania, but maybe that's good. If I can hack it in the coldest, darkest time of the year, I can hack it anytime. And maybe you can, too.

Wednesday, November 14. The last day I'll be driving to work for a while. On the way home I top off the van's 20-gallon tank, paying $1.39 per gallon for regular unleaded. Let's see if I can survive a month without buying more.

At noon I do a dry run on the Cannondale mountain bike I modified for commuting. Fitted with fenders, lights, a rear rack, and an aero handlebar extension for more hand positions, it's heavy and ungainly but ready for business. I dub it the Cannonball.

The test ride to my house and back has me smiling. My position and the handling are fine. And surprisingly, no rattles. I'm also glad to see a round-trip average speed of 16 mph despite the bike's 38 pounds and the route's 1,400 feet of elevation gain. This might not be too bad.

The First-Day Jitters

Thursday, November 15. There couldn't be a better morning to begin—38°F, light tailwind, rising sun strobing golden through the trees. But before leaving the house at 7:10, it takes more minutes than I figured to select office clothes and put them into the rack-top pack. I decide it would be better to do this each evening to save time. A rolled shirt and pants probably won't be any more wrinkled after 12 hours than they are after one. (The way I iron, they might even look better.)

I arrive at the office in 42 minutes—12.5 primarily downhill miles at 18 mph. I hang the bike inside and start walking upstairs before realizing the pack with my clothes is still on the rack. (Gee, I didn't count on having to think.) After a quick shower, I dress in clothes that are still cool, a nice feeling. It's 8:20 when I turn on my computer to begin work. That's an hour later than usual, but a lot of the time has been used for exercise.

At 5:15 P.M. I see a beautiful coral sky outside the west window, but my heart is sinking with the sun. I'm 12 miles from home without the van, facing almost an hour of pedaling in the dark. I'm surprised by the apprehension I feel. After 20 years of cycling, this will be my first night ride.

Hey, no problem! I'm using the highly rated Nightsun light system, and it's well named. Oncoming drivers dim their brights as if I'm another auto, and I can see road signs glowing 200 feet ahead. When climbing I switch off the high beam to save the rechargeable battery, and the low one is plenty at slow speed. Meanwhile, the blinking amber taillight causes overtaking cars to slow and give me plenty of room. After 20 minutes, I feel a lot more confident.

Minor Adjustments

Friday, November 16. At 6:45 A.M., just 11 hours after climbing off the bike, I'm back on. I was up in time to leave earlier but decided to wait for enough light to see the road and surroundings. Coming home last night was fun, but one dark ride each day is enough.

Saturday, November 17. Looking out at a cold rain, I thank my luck. No commute today. I decide that Saturday mornings will be when I use the van to drive to town for appointments, errands, and the week's groceries. Today it takes 37 miles and five stops to accomplish everything on my list.

Normally I'm fairly organized, but bike commuting is already making me plan better and stick to my schedule. For instance, one of my stops today was to pick up a supply of disposable contact lenses across town. Considering the rain and traffic, I almost decided to wait. Then I remembered I wouldn't have the van at work, and cycling wouldn't be very pleasant because of the optometrist's location. When his secretary asked me to schedule my annual exam, I picked a Saturday for the same reasons.

Choosing the Right Bike

Monday, November 19. At 7:10 A.M. it's clear, breezy, and 27°F, which is the same as 0 at 18 mph. I'm comfortable wearing the winter garb I use for training rides, thus sparing the expense of buying anything additional for commuting. The only problem is the extra minutes it takes to dress and undress twice a day at this time of year.

And now, after seven trips, a word about my commuter bike: great. I'm congratulating myself for choosing a mountain bike instead of a road model. The granny chainring is a godsend when pedaling 230 pounds (bike and well-clothed body) up the hills. It means I never have to strain, which lets me baby my cold body during the initial miles and keeps sweat to a minimum in subfreezing temperatures. More important, it removes the mental blocks that can build when certain parts of each ride are a grind. When you're doing 1,400 vertical feet a day, that's important.

Of course, a road bike can have a granny ring, too, but I think a mountain (or perhaps hybrid) bike is still better. An incident this morning explains why. I'd just descended into town and was on a narrow, curvy, rolling section of road when a dump truck with a trailer pulled up to my left elbow, ready to do something stupid. Just ahead I spotted a gravel shoulder and, without hesitation, turned onto it and braked slightly, letting the truck rumble past. As I steered over the lip back onto the pavement, my bike choice had been validated. No matter what might happen during the month, I knew the Cannonball could handle it.

Experimenting with Clothing

Tuesday, November 20. Hey, I'm feeling in the groove. Good weather, steady pedaling, and continuous amazement at how much room overtaking traffic gives me at night. I wish there were a way to get the same respect from drivers in daylight.

Wednesday, November 21. During my commute last night and again this morning, I wear a $200 high-tech jacket made with one of those miracle fabrics. You know, the kind that blocks wind and water while allowing body heat to escape, thus keeping you warm and dry. Right. At the end of each ride, my polypropylene turtleneck (the only thing under the jacket despite freezing temperatures) is saturated, including the sleeves. By comparison, on previous rides in my old Italian-made cycling jacket (50 percent wool/50 percent acrylic with low-tech nylon wind panels on the chest and arms), the same turtleneck gets only a damp spot on the upper back. Maybe I'll try the expensive model again when it rains.

The Slimming Aspects

Thursday, November 22. Thanksgiving morning, a time when I traditionally take a long ride to enjoy traffic-free roads and earn a calorie-laden feast. I feel so good on my road bike that I extend the route from 50 to 67 miles, and I would have gone farther if I'd taken a second energy bar. I'm happy knowing that riding the Cannonball isn't somehow killing my legs (or enthusiasm) for long road rides, my favorite type of cycling. Curiously, though, it seems to be making me lose weight even though I'm eating well and riding no more each day than I normally would. To learn if this is something inherent in cycling twice a day (and apt to affect other bike commuters), I ask three members of *Bicycling*'s Fitness Advisory Board. They tell me that each 45-minute commute is elevating my metabolism for about 6 hours. Therefore, riding to work and back keeps me (and would keep you) burning extra calories for 12 hours each day, in addition to those used during riding.

Office Pros and Cons

Tuesday, November 27. I was tired last night but still didn't get to bed until 11:30. When the coffeemaker clicks on at 5:45 this morning, I don't want to get up. This attitude stays with me through breakfast, shaving, dressing, and pedaling up the driveway. But soon, cruising through calm air under a winter-gray sky, I begin to feel better. By the time I reach the office, I'm pumped. Would my mood have changed so much in 12 miles if I'd been behind a steering wheel? It never did before.

Thursday, November 29. Again I feel supercharged as I hang up the bike and walk to my office. There really is something about an early-morning workout that can become addictive. Then, uh oh, I find my door locked (the janitor did it by mistake), and I don't have a key. Hurry, call maintenance and hope they can break me in quickly because I'm due at a meeting in 25 minutes. This gives me time to consider a drawback of commuting: After arriving in cycling clothes and a light sweat, you're still a ways from being ready for the job. Today, though, I get to the meeting with 2 minutes to spare.

Reducing Driving Mileage

Friday, November 30. There are long lines at gas stations this evening as people of questionable intelligence seek one more tankful before tomorrow's 5-cent-per-gallon increase in the federal gas tax. Think about it: They wait in line for 15 minutes with the engine idling in order to save 60 cents on a typical 12-gallon fill up. I can laugh because my van still has about 16 of those 20 gallons it contained 15 days ago.

Saturday, December 1. I do my errands in a sequence that keeps driving mileage to a minimum. One stop is my office, where I put a week's worth of clothes into my file cabinet's empty drawer. I'm tired of the tediousness of packing and unpacking each day, so I'll try it this way instead.

Facing Harsh Weather

Monday, December 3. Up early to read some manuscripts and edit an article before riding in. The weather radio calls for rain by afternoon, then windy and cold for the rest of the week. Shortly after 7:00, I wheel the Cannonball out the door and—surprise—step into a shower of frozen rain. "The party's over," I think as I pedal up the driveway, headlight blazing in the dank dawn. Soon a school bus overtakes me and every kid is pressed against the rear window, agog at the sight. Within 2 miles the sleet stops and the road dries. I may not be so lucky this afternoon.

I'm not. It's raining steadily, getting foggy, and a blustery wind is whipping in from the south, boosting the temperature into the 50s. It's a light day at work, so I leave at 4:00 P.M. in order to get home before dark. I haven't used my light in a soaking rain yet, and I'm worried that it might short out and leave me stranded. But it works fine.

The same can't be said for the rainsuit I try. Yeah, it keeps the water out, but it's so hot inside I get wet anyway. I'm panting on hills and holding my face into the rain for relief. I can understand using these high-tech materials on the front of pants and jackets to block wind and water, but a cyclist generates too much heat to be fully enclosed.

A rainy-day commute doesn't end when you get home, of course, because bike cleanup and lubrication takes another 5 to 10 minutes. The rack pack has leaked a bit, but thanks to a zip-close plastic bag my homework is dry. After a shower, I work at my PC for a couple of hours to compensate for the lost office time. If this is what it takes to be a bike commuter, I don't mind.

Tuesday, December 4. The cold front arrives as predicted, driving down the temperature with a hard northwest wind. By 7:00 P.M. it's in the low 30s and I ride through snow flurries. This time I try a jacket—isn't it great to work for a bike magazine?—with Gore-Tex front panels, fleece lining, and a fabric back to vent body heat. It works pretty well. I also like the fleece-lined stretch tights with a windproof nylon front. Best of all are the lightweight, fleece-lined, stretch Gore-Tex booties, the only type I've used that match thick neoprene's warmth but don't cause condensation. They should be even better in the wet because Gore-Tex, unlike neoprene, is waterproof.

Despite winter's gloom, *Bicycling* editor Ed Pavelka found riding to work
an enlightening experience.

Wednesday, December 5. The picture for this chapter is being taken this morning, which dawns at a blustery 28°F. Meanwhile, a new element enters the commute: ice. There are numerous patches where runoff from yesterday morning's heavy rain has frozen. All I can do is ride straight across and hope not to slip.

Monday, December 10. By nightfall a cold northwest wind is surging. At 8:15 I head for home. On the first climb, leaves blow past me as if I'm standing still. In fact, I almost am, since a busy weekend and a long workday have left me tired. But I pedal on in my bubble of light, one stroke at a time, buffeted in the darkness. It's hard, and when I finally reach the house I feel good about myself.

Adjusting Work Schedules

Tuesday, December 11. I brought home an article to edit last night, but it got too late. So I tackle it at 5:30 this morning while sipping coffee, eating oatmeal, and waiting for the sun to rise. Click! Why not plan to work more at home so I can leave the office at a reasonable time? I make it my goal, beginning today, to be showered and at the office no later than 8:30 A.M. and on the road home by 4:30 P.M.

True to this schedule, I'm weight-trained, showered, and fed by 7:30 P.M. and sitting at the home computer, where I give a couple of productive hours to the magazine and one to myself. Yeah, this is the way to do it. If you, too, have some flexibility in your office schedule and can do parts of your job at home, commuting may fit more easily into your life than you think.

An Added Benefit

Wednesday, December 12. Hey, it's already day 18. Riding to work seems normal, ingrained. At the office I call my car insurance agent to inquire what would happen to my premium if the van's status were changed from "more than 7,500 miles per year for work" to "less than 7,500 for pleasure." The answer: an annual savings of $108. I tell him to do it.

Socializing and Riding

Thursday, December 13. Tonight I get the chance to try something different. We're having our staff Christmas party at an editor's house, which not only means I'll be riding home later, but I'll also be doing it with a full stomach.

Because I'm in my riding clothes, I get some cocktail party-type questions about how commuting is going, will I continue doing it, blah, blah, and isn't it dangerous to ride at night? The answers: great, yes, and it may be safer. I'm so well lit and reflectorized that drivers are extra cautious. I haven't had a close call and, in fact, have heard only one horn, which I interpreted as friendly.

The ride home is against the wind. My gut is stuffed with everything from pizza to raw vegetables, topped by two or three (or ten) killer chocolate-chip cookies. I even drank a few beers, but stopped 90 minutes before it was time to leave. Thanks again to the Cannonball's low gears, I'm able to minimize exertion on climbs, which spares my stomach but doesn't do much for my headache. I shower and go straight to bed.

Friday, December 14. I awake feeling bloated. Coffee doesn't perk me up, and I eat some oatmeal even though I have no appetite. I climb on the bike with less enthusiasm than I've had in a long time and pedal into the subfreezing, semidark morning.

Well, you can guess the rest of the story. When I arrive at the office 48 minutes later I feel like Clark Kent exiting a phone booth. Judging by the condition of some of the other staffers, however, I don't think this transformation would have happened if, like them, I'd driven in.

The ride home is the final commute planned for this experiment, but it's not the last. I'm into it. I figure the only thing that can stop me is ice and snow. Around here, this won't mean too many days off the bike.

The True Savings and Bonuses

Saturday, December 15. We know that commuting by bike saves natural resources and protects the air, but obviously this isn't enough to get many people started. So let's see what it means to something really important: your money.

This morning, 30 days after removing my van from everyday use, I drive to the gas station. It takes 8.8 gallons to refill the tank. The tab is $12.70, so this is what it cost for all the driving necessary in a month. Meanwhile, I commuted 500 miles by bike, which spared 26 gallons worth $37.50 at today's price. This extends to an annual savings of $450 (plus $108 in lower insurance premiums). Then there's the reduced wear and maintenance that results from driving 6,000 fewer miles per year. Not only will this double the van's remaining life, but it'll do so at no additional expense.

Considering all this, plus the fitness and enjoyment that result from riding at least 25 miles per day, it's a shame it took me so long to try bike commuting. But now that I have, I'm looking forward to the benefits for years to come.

2 NO EXCUSES, ONLY SOLUTIONS

The only valid reason not to commute by bicycle is that you don't want to. But that's nothing to feel guilty about. Some people enjoy staring through their windshield twice a day at the back of another motorist's head. And lots of cyclists are content to ride only on weekends. They never aspire to improve their fitness or increase their weekly mileage.

Complete this sentence: "I'd like to be a bicycle commuter, but. . . ." Now watch how easy it is to shoot holes through these excuses. Here are the solutions to every problem you may be anticipating.

Equipment

Excuse: I can't afford a special commuter bike.

Solution: You don't need one. Even a racing bike can be fitted with a light alloy rack and a pack big enough to hold a change of clothes. Wearing a small backpack or fannypack is another option. Sure, it's great to have a special all-weather bike with fenders, lights, a front rack, panniers, sturdy wheels, and Kevlar-belted touring tires. But if your commuting will be done only in daylight and rarely in the rain, an inexpensive, used "beater" bike is better than a shiny new one, assuming you maintain it properly. You won't feel obligated to wash it every time it gets dirty, and each scratch won't make you nauseous. It also won't be the envy of every bike thief.

Dressing for Work

Excuse: I have to dress well for work and can't stuff my good clothes in panniers.

Solution: Drive to work on Fridays, leave a week's worth of clean clothes, and take the dirty stuff home. Why Friday? Because for some reason motorists seem to be less tolerant of cyclists on Friday afternoons. Driving also gives you a rest before your longer weekend rides, and it provides a chance to knock off a couple of errands that are accomplished more easily by car. Increase your efficiency by getting in the habit of scheduling personal appointments, shopping, and other side trips for Fridays.

If your commute is a short one, simply wear your office clothes. Drivers may even be more careful if you're dressed like a lawyer.

Showering

Excuse: I can't shower at work.
Solution: Store a washcloth, soap, towel, and deodorant in your office. Clean up at the restroom sink. Or, check for a nearby health club, school, or hotel that may provide a locker and shower.

Bike Theft

Excuse: There's no secure place to park my bike.
Solution: Most buildings have a storage closet or out-of-the-way corner somewhere. If you can't secure your bike behind a locked door or put it where you can see it, fasten it to an immovable object with a stout U-lock. If your boss won't allow your bike in the workplace, find a sympathetic co-worker who lives nearby, a bike shop, or another place within walking distance. Free storage is ideal, but a few bucks' rent is cheap insurance to make sure your bike will be waiting for the ride home.

Rush-Hour Danger

Excuse: It's not safe to ride in rush-hour traffic.
Solution: Not if your route to work is the San Diego Freeway. But it's usually possible to get from point A to point B on quiet city streets or secondary roads. Scout a route on your bike during the weekend when traffic is light and you can try several alternatives. Or you can do it on the kitchen table using a city map obtained in a bookstore. To commute on a less-congested route you may travel a few extra miles, but the point is to be safe and enjoy your ride. And more miles bring more fitness.

Unless you're sharing the road with New York City buses and cabs, the fear of riding in traffic is often disproportionate to the actual danger. In stop-and-go traffic, a fit cyclist can usually maintain the same speed as cars, so it's acceptable to ride in the traffic lane instead of hugging the curb where you're less visible. If you don't claim your rightful place on the road, you'll tempt even mild-mannered motorists to squeeze past. Look at it this way—if they're honking at you, at least they see you.

To share the road successfully with cars, always ride lawfully, assertively, predictably, and where you're visible. This means riding where motorists expect to see other vehicles. Books have been written on the subject (and so has part 2 of this book), but one example illustrates this point exactly: When preparing to make a left turn, don't hug the right shoulder until the last second so you have to dart across lanes of overtaking traffic. Instead, signal your intention and get to the left early. A rearview mirror will help you choose the right moment, but always glance behind to double-check. And always wear a helmet.

Losing Sleep

Excuse: I like to sleep. I'd have to get up earlier if I rode my bike.

Solution: Because of traffic, you can usually cycle from home to work in about the same time it takes to drive. If you subtract the time it takes to find a parking spot but add the time to clean up and change clothes, you're still almost equal. Besides, those few extra minutes of sleep aren't nearly as refreshing as a brisk morning ride. You'll arrive at work invigorated. And your evening ride home will leave you relaxed, so you'll sleep more soundly. Quality over quantity.

Long Work Hours

Excuse: I leave for work early and come home late. I'd have to ride in the dark.

Solution: Wear light-colored, reflective clothing, and attach lights and reflectors. Even most thoroughfares won't be busy before and after rush hour, and for some reason drivers tend to be more careful when overtaking a cyclist in the dark. If your route is lined with streetlights that provide ample illumination, aim your headlight at drivers' eye level so oncoming traffic will be sure to notice you. If you ride on unlit rural roads, use a dual-beam headlight so you can switch to high when there's no ambient light.

Foul Weather

Excuse: I don't like riding in the cold/rain/snow.
Solution: Don't. Just because some commuters bare themselves to nature's fury by riding every day doesn't mean you have to. But even if the weather is clement only half the year, that's a lot of gas you'll save and fitness you'll build. And who knows, you may start looking forward to your daily rides so much you'll invest in a rainsuit and cold-weather attire. One thing is almost always true: The weather is never as terrible for cycling as it seems through the window of your cozy home or office.

Too Many Miles

Excuse: My commute is too far to ride.
Solution: Tell it to Pete Penseyres, former winner of the Race Across America (RAAM). He commutes at least 30 miles each way when he's training. But if you're that far from work and not up to rising at 6:00 A.M. for a 2-hour ride, consider cycling only partway. Drive within range, park, and pedal the rest. If leaving your car isn't convenient, maybe you can take the bus or train to where your bike is stashed.

Too Few Miles

Excuse: I live too close to work to make riding worthwhile.
Solution: Take the long way. Let's say you live 5 miles from the office. When the weather is cold or rainy, that's plenty of riding. But for better days, create routes that extend the ride in or out to 10, 15, or more miles, thus combining training with commuting.

Reaction from Co-Workers

Excuse: People will think I'm weird if I ride a bike to work.
Solution: Actually, those days are past. Your co-workers are much more likely to understand and respect your interest in fitness and protecting the environment. An increasing percentage of motorists will see it this way, too, because more U.S. adults than ever include cycling as one of their recreational activities. Lots more people behind a steering wheel know it isn't strange to be behind a handlebar.

A Car Is Necessary

Excuse: I need my car for work.
Solution: It's tough to shoot holes in this argument. You probably don't want to leave your car at the office, but it's a possibility if you have two. Another idea is to schedule car-related work for certain days and commute by bike on the others. Or, see how realistic it might be to use your bike for work trips instead of your car. If you try, there may be a way to commute by bike one or two days a week, which still adds up to a worthwhile amount of cycling each year.

Part Two

SHARING THE ROAD WITH MOTOR VEHICLES

3 ■ END YOUR FEAR OF RIDING IN TRAFFIC

After reading the first two chapters, you're almost convinced to become a bicycle commuter. We've punctured your excuses and shown you how getting started won't require major lifestyle changes. But if you're like most cyclists contemplating city streets with rush-hour traffic, you still have concerns about safety. That's good. A healthy respect for motor vehicles is necessary, but it doesn't mean you should ride apprehensively. You won't after reading this chapter (and the four others also included in part 2), which includes many tips by experts and cyclists like you about riding urban roadways and dealing with drivers.

Tips on Staying Safe

You ride a bike for fun and fitness, and now you're thinking of using it to get to work and back. But every time you consider riding in traffic twice a day you're immobilized by thoughts of hurtling cars and trucks, potholes, and road rash.

Congratulations—you're 100 percent normal! But your fear of riding in traffic is neither foolish nor incurable. Learning a few simple tips can transform you from a road worrier to a road warrior.

An estimated 88 million Americans ride bikes, but industry experts say no more than 10 million do it weekly. Some may simply be lazy or uninterested, but it's a safe bet that many are just plain apprehensive. The main thing to understand is that cyclists belong on the road. "You have the same [basic] rights and responsibilities as cars in all 50 states," notes Arlene Plevin, former editor of *Bicycle USA,* a magazine published by the League of American Wheelmen. "You have the right to be there."

Face Your Fears

Realizing this means overcoming the "traffic inferiority complex," a term used by John Forester, founder of a nationwide instructional program called Effective Cycling. "You'll never do it right until you feel deep down inside that you are as important as motorists," Forester writes in his handbook.

What's more, your misgivings may be based on some misconceptions. For new riders, "The most common fear is being hit from behind by a car," says Steven Gottlieb, an Effective Cycling instructor in Bloomington, Indiana. But only a small fraction of cycling accidents happen this way. In fact, car/bike collisions of any kind account for only 12 percent of all cycling mishaps, according to one study. Far more common are accidents in which riders simply fall off their bikes, typically because they hit road debris or try to stop too fast.

Act Like a Car

Even so, cars can be hazardous. The best way to keep them at bay is to act like one. "Obey the vehicular laws," advises Gottlieb. "Some adults ride the same way they did when they were kids. They don't recognize that vehicular rules apply to cyclists."

This means cycling with traffic instead of against it, riding in a straight line, obeying stop signs and traffic lights, using hand signals when turning, making left turns from the left side of the lane (or the turning lane), and using lights when riding at night. What's more, you should keep right to allow cars to pass, but don't ride so far over that motorists forget you have a right to your share of pavement. Riding on the road edge encourages motorists to turn right in front of you and makes you less visible to cars entering from side streets. (See chapter 4 for details on how to ride in traffic.)

Watch for Road Hazards

Other tips include watching for hazards such as railroad tracks (which you should cross at a right angle) and riding two abreast only on quiet back roads (and where legal). Avoid offensive words or gestures that can inflame drivers, heed pedestrians and runners, wear brightly colored clothing when visibility is poor, keep your bike in good working order, and carry identification and emergency telephone numbers. And *always* wear a helmet.

Practice Drills
for Moving Like Traffic

Armed with knowledge of your rights and responsibilities, you're ready to put the rubber to the road. But don't rush to the busiest intersection to practice. Learn to master traffic one step at a time.

Yvonne Morrison, an Effective Cycling instructor at Arizona State University in Tempe, uses a three-stage traffic-indoctrination approach. After classroom sessions on topics such as accident statistics and road position, she takes her charges for a ride in a lightly trafficked residential area. Here, they practice looking behind without swerving and making right and left turns.

Next, Morrison takes students to a "collector"—a moderately busy four-way intersection with a traffic light. Here, they learn how to turn left from single and left-turn-only lanes. Then the class graduates to pedaling on minor arterial roads. Morrison also conducts a "left-turn ride," where "every time they can turn left, they have to do it."

"I don't go into this type of thing lightly," explains Morrison, who's been teaching the course for a decade. However, she notes that students "find out that it's not as hard as it looks." They quickly become comfortable in traffic.

Protecting Yourself
from Drivers' Errors

Mastering all the above skills will make you a competent cyclist and enhance your safety on the road. But this doesn't mean you can completely relax. After all, anyone can get into accidents caused by bad drivers. To protect yourself, you need to practice defensive cycling.

The first step is to be aware of the dangers. According to Gottlieb, three of the most common driver errors that threaten cyclists are:

- Turning left in front of an oncoming cyclist who's going straight through an intersection.
- Failing to obey a stop sign and pulling in front of a rider.
- Passing a cyclist and immediately turning right across his or her path.

Stay Aware

To guard against these hazards, Gottlieb advises, "Be aware of what cars around you are doing." Is an oncoming car slowing but not signaling? It may be preparing to turn in front of you. Is a truck creeping out from a side street? Don't assume the driver sees you. (Try to establish eye contact.) If you have the right-of-way at an intersection, don't coast through or drivers may assume they can cut in front of you. Keep pedaling, but be prepared to brake.

Use your ears as an early warning system. Tip-offs to danger include engines revving or slowing, squealing tires, and gear changes. (See the section "Be Alert" on page 32 for more on potential hazards.)

Master
Emergency Maneuvers

Gottlieb also recommends practicing emergency maneuvers such as a panic stop. Be sure to apply both brakes simultaneously, though you should emphasize the front one because it's more powerful. Using only the front brake may send you over the handlebar, and using only the rear won't stop you fast enough. To counter the bike's tendency to pivot forward over the front wheel, slide off the back of the saddle with arms extended. (See the photo on page 24.)

Another useful skill is the "instant turn." This evasive action comes in handy when a car passes you and immediately turns right, or when an oncoming car turns left across your path, leaving you no time to brake. Steer left briefly to create a lean angle, then immediately turn right with the car to avoid a collision. (See the illustration on the opposite page.)

When applying both front and rear brakes at the same time in an emergency stop, keep your weight well to the rear to prevent pitchover.

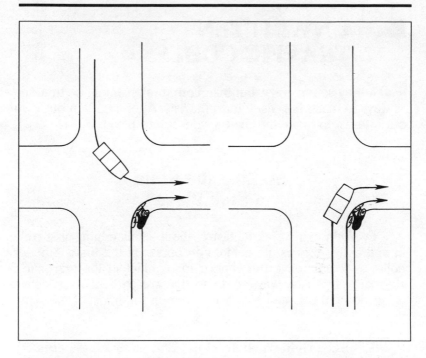

When opposing or overtaking traffic suddenly turns in front of you, steer left briefly to create a lean angle, then turn with the vehicle to avoid a collision.

Ride with Confidence

Once you're able to do all this, you can ride even the busiest roads with confidence. It's merely a matter of knowing a few rules and tricks, having the proper equipment, and using common sense. Says Gottlieb: "I tell my Effective Cycling students, 'Use your head first. When all else fails, rely on your helmet.'"

(Effective Cycling is a nationwide instructional program that teaches the craft of cycling. The program is administered by the League of American Wheelmen. For more information, send a SASE to LAW, 6707 Whitestone Road, Baltimore, MD 21207.)

◼️4 UNWRITTEN TRAFFIC CODES

It may sound crazy, but bike commuters should be thinking of ways to make life easier for motorists. After all, it's in our own self-interest to make the road a safer, more pleasant place.

Making the Road a Safe Place

Even though we all fantasize about retaliating against rude or aggressive drivers, it's seldom an option at the time. A better policy is to minimize the chance for conflict in the first place. Here are eight easy ways to do so that are particularly effective when riding the same roads daily, often in the midst of the same drivers.

1.   Keep right when possible. Stay as far left as necessary for your safety, but if there's a wide, clean shoulder, use it. Barring potholes, storm grates, parked cars, glass, and other hazards, most of the time it's easier (and safer) to ride to the right. One thing that always irritates motorists is a cyclist riding well into the middle of the roadway for no apparent reason. Besides, why take unnecessary risks? You can never be sure the driver behind you isn't a short-fused nut.

2.   Use common sense about riding two or more abreast. It's enjoyable to ride side-by-side with a companion and carry on a conversation. This can make it much more interesting when regularly riding the same route. But road and traffic conditions may be such that vehicles back up behind you when they could otherwise get by. Thus, restrict side-by-side riding to quiet, secondary roads or when you're using a wide shoulder.

3.   Don't force vehicles to repass you needlessly. This always bears repeating. Let's say you're riding along a narrow, busy road and motorists are having trouble getting by you. There's half a dozen cars waiting at the next red light, all of which have already patiently overtaken you. Do you maintain your place in line, or do you zip past everyone on the right so you'll get the jump when the light changes? If you do the latter, you might gain 50 feet and save a few seconds, but you'll also probably create six antibicyclists when they get caught behind you again.

Admittedly, the scenario becomes trickier if, by hanging back, you miss the light. There are two tactful ways around this. One is to only move up in line far enough to just make the light. The other is to ride to the light, but move out slowly and slightly to the right when it turns green, letting the cars through the intersection first. One other courtesy at traffic lights: Avoid blocking drivers who want to turn right on red.

4. Ride predictably. This one's easy. Ride in a straight line when you're cruising, and use hand signals when turning or changing lanes. If you're riding erratically, it's difficult for drivers to know when to pass. They may let several relatively safe opportunities go by before becoming exasperated and taking a dangerous chance.

Hand signals are a courtesy and an important part of safe cycling. Motorists feel more comfortable dealing with cyclists who communicate their intentions. More important, drivers tend to show them more respect.

5. Avoid busy roads. If you commute on a busy highway, you'll risk ruffling the delicate feathers of already edgy drivers. But an alternate route doesn't have to be a residential street with stop signs every quarter mile, or a glass-littered, jogger-strewn bike path. Examine a detailed map of your area and you'll probably be surprised at the many relatively quiet roads that'll get you where you need to go.

6. Make yourself visible. In conditions where motorists might not readily see you (an overcast day, for example), it's a courtesy and plain good sense to wear brightly colored clothes. Drivers will never blame themselves when they almost pull into your path after a too-casual look. Unfair, yes; but you can greatly enhance your safety by dressing to be seen. At night, it's a different story. Drivers who encounter cyclists riding without lights and reflectors are right to consider them menaces.

7. Be careful about "provocative" actions. At a red light, even friendly drivers are likely to be irritated by a cyclist riding in circles in front of them. Many view it as a challenge to their right-of-way, even when none is intended. Similarly, if you lean on a vehicle at a stoplight, be aware that most drivers consider their cars extensions of themselves. You wouldn't want someone leaning on your bike, would you?

8. Return the favor. Cyclists come to appreciate little unexpected courtesies from motorists. For instance, we all nod a thank you to the driver who has the right of way but waves us through anyway. Try returning the favor. You might, for example, motion a driver to make his turn in front of you if you'll be slow getting under way. Who knows? That driver might look a bit more favorably on the next cyclist down the road.

 MANEUVERS FOR CITY CYCLING

Rush-hour traffic, to any cyclist who has not experienced it, can be a cacophony of blowing horns and revving engines, a life-threatening maelstrom of two-ton projectiles piloted erratically by glowering maniacs or myopic, pea-brained dullards.

But there is a method to all this internal-combustion madness. Those scowling drivers aren't out to get you, they just want to get to work or home, and you're on their turf, delaying them for precious seconds. Despite their rudeness, most motorists are law-abiding citizens, and the few who aren't realize that running you over would only cause further delay.

Books have been written on the techniques of dealing with every conceivable traffic situation. John S. Allen's *The Complete Book of Bicycle Commuting* and John Forester's *Effective Cycling* are particularly useful. But the whole trick of surviving in traffic can be reduced to three basic rules:

1. Be seen.
2. Be predictable.
3. Be alert.

Be Seen

Motorists are programmed to be alert for other cars, not for bicycles. Help them notice you by wearing bright colors such as red, yellow, and orange, and use lights and reflectors before sunrise or after sundown. Reflective helmet covers and clothing are also very effective.

Ride Where Drivers
Expect to See You

More basic, though, is using that part of the roadway where motorists expect to see traffic. This begins with never riding against the flow. This isn't just because a head-on collision is more serious than getting hit from behind or sideswiped; motorists pulling out from side streets don't expect vehicles to approach from the "wrong" direction.

If you're giving parked cars enough berth to avoid suddenly opening doors (and children darting into the street), you may attract some angry honks from following motorists who don't understand why you won't pull right to let them pass. Riders welcome those honks as acknowledgments that drivers see them and aren't going to hit them. Given the choice between delaying a motor vehicle—ambulances, fire trucks, and police cars excepted—a few seconds and crashing into an open car door at 18 mph, the honker's momentary inconvenience is a better choice every time.

Wait for a Red Light

While waiting for a red light behind a long line of stopped traffic, we've all been tempted to gain ground by passing on the right, between the cars and the curb (perhaps lined with cars that are parallel parked). Don't do it. It's illegal and you can get "doored" from either side. Also, if the traffic starts moving, someone may veer or turn right, never suspecting that you are coming up. Wait your turn in line, just like a car.

But it works the other way, too. When you stop for a light, move to the center of the lane to await the green. This prevents vehicles from edging forward, trapping you between them and the curb. You're not being inconsiderate, since you can easily accelerate with the traffic. As soon as you reach cruising speed, move right and allow the following cars to pass.

Use the Traffic Lane

While most states require you to ride as far to the right as safe and practicable, there are times you'll want to occupy the center of the traffic lane for visibility's sake. For example, one commuter who rides through several busy intersections en route to and from work each day faces the very real danger of an oncoming motorist suddenly turning left, into his path. To help prevent this, he rides in the center of the traffic lane through these crossings, so drivers waiting to turn can easily spot him. If he hugged the shoulder he'd make people behind him happier, but he'd become all but invisible.

Be Predictable

Motorists (at least sober ones) don't steer their cars in and out of the spaces between parallel-parked vehicles, they don't swerve suddenly across lanes of traffic without signaling, and they don't pull out of side streets without stopping to look for oncoming traffic. If you're going to join the fray on your two-wheeled vehicle, you shouldn't either.

As when you're behind the wheel, the best advice when cycling in the city is to ride defensively. This doesn't mean timidly. Be predictable, and go about your business with a self-assurance that shows. When motorists feel comfortable with you, there is less chance they'll do something that puts you in danger.

Ride a Straight Line

By riding in a straight line along the edge of the road, you're showing drivers how far left they'll need to steer to pass you safely. But suddenly weave left and that safe passing distance is reduced to zero. Bam, you've just been hit, and it's your fault. So keep your eyes on the road ahead, and anticipate the need for any avoidance maneuvers as early as possible.

If you see a pothole ahead, don't wait until the last possible second to swoop around it. After looking over your left shoulder (in itself a signal to drivers behind) and holding out your left hand to indicate an imminent movement in that direction, steer gradually to the left until your forward path is clear of the pothole. Then, just as smoothly, steer right and continue your straight-line riding.

Although drivers might love you to veer toward the curb and allow them to pass every time there's an empty space between parked cars, don't do it. You may be providing extra passing room, but what happens when you approach the rear bumper of the next parked car? You swerve left, directly into the path of someone who hasn't allowed extra room for a cyclist. It's better to steer a straight course past parked cars and empty spaces, allowing drivers to gauge the passing room they need.

Use Hand Signals

By making liberal use of hand signals for turns, swerves, and braking maneuvers, you'll let cars know what you're up to. You'll also earn some respect as a conscientious user of the road. You can use your left arm to signal left turns (index finger pointing) and braking (palm facing backward), and use your right arm for right turns. That business about signaling right turns with your left arm comes from an old rule motorists followed, because one can't exactly reach across and stick his hand out the right window. It doesn't apply to cyclists.

Be Alert

Every high school defensive driving course should include several rush-hour sessions on a bicycle. Exposed to the dangers of dodging automobiles and trucks, you sharpen your senses and learn to spot potential dangers long before a daydreaming driver surrounded by 90 decibels of four-channel sound.

Look
for Potential Hazards

Since most potential hazards appear to your front, learn to scrutinize each side street and driveway for cars, kids on bikes, dogs, runaway shopping carts, or whatever. Also look through the rear windows of parked cars for someone who might throw open a door or a pedestrian about to step out from between cars.

Just because a car is stopped at a cross street, don't expect it to remain stopped until you pass. Books on bicycle safety often recommend making eye contact with drivers to be sure you're seen, but some motorists can look directly at you and still pull out. Either they think you're supposed to give them the right of way or they underestimate your speed. So it's a good idea to watch the front wheels, where it's possible to spot even slight forward movement. If you see any, get ready to brake, swerve, and/or shout.

Shout!

Forget horns, bells, and whistles as warning devices. The time you spend searching for the horn button or putting the whistle to your lips is better spent avoiding the hazard. A powerful shout originating deep in your diaphragm is just as loud, quicker to execute, and requires no hands.

Watch
for Sudden Right Turns

Although we've been advising you to worry about cars ahead, not behind, there is one common bike/car collision caused by following motorists—the sudden right turn. For some exasperating reason, drivers all too frequently overtake a cyclist and immediately make a right turn with no consideration for the fate of the rider. When this happens it's time for hard braking. When it happens before the rear fender has passed you, you've got no choice but to turn with it.

This hazard occurs almost entirely in the morning, as half-dozing drivers make their way to work. Be especially wary on Monday mornings. Afternoons find motorists more alert, but also more aggressive. They're less apt to tolerate a second's delay to ensure your safe passage. Friday afternoons and any weekday afternoon before a holiday, when everyone's hurrying to start their mini-vacations, are when drivers seem to be least courteous.

█ 6 █ SIMPLE STEPS FOR AVOIDING ACCIDENTS

Bob Katz is a social worker and cyclist in Toronto. His practice serves seriously disabled accident victims, and a number of his clients were hurt in incidents where the motorized vehicle was at fault. "Big deal," says Katz. "Being right isn't much compensation if you can't ride anymore. No judge has ever awarded a cyclist a new spinal cord."

Here's good advice: Forget all the rules of traffic etiquette you ever learned. The average bicycle weighs 25 pounds. The average motorized vehicle weighs 2,500 pounds. Your job is to avoid getting into an accident, not to prove you were within your rights after you've been involved in one. In this chapter, Katz explains the consequences some riders have faced when they didn't behave like traffic.

Accidents That Shouldn't Have Happened

Most cyclists know the importance of wearing a helmet, being visible, and obeying traffic laws. Unfortunately, this isn't enough to guard against common bike/vehicle accidents. To do so, you must be predictable and properly positioned.

Here are some real accidents involving cyclists. Although each rider was being cautious and was not at fault, each incident could have been avoided had he or she been acting more like traffic.

- John is riding as far to the right as practical when he is overtaken by a van. A few seconds later, the van makes a right turn without signaling and he smashes into its front fender.
- Mary is cycling close to a row of parked cars when suddenly a door opens in her path. There isn't time to react, and she crashes into it.
- Bill is riding in the right lane when the car in front of him begins to slow. As he applies the brakes, his front

wheel drops into a vertical sewer grate and he flips over the handlebar.
- Joan is cycling in the gutter when a small truck passes too close to her. Its right rearview mirror strikes her helmet, knocking her from the bike.

Too Far to the Right

In each of these incidents the cyclists were riding too far to the right. Drivers usually won't move over for a cyclist in this position. Instead, they attempt to squeeze by or ignore the cyclist entirely. In each case the correct riding technique would have been to do as traffic does and occupy a greater share of the road.

Although drivers won't be pleased when they have to slow and wait for an opportunity to pass, your safety is more important than their next appointment. Riding to the extreme right makes you less visible and less a part of traffic. In fact, the space behind a car's left or right fender is called the "blind spot." Only a fool wants to be there.

Gaining a Wide Berth

A few months ago I did an experiment while cycling on a 40-mph, limited-access road in Toronto. Normally, I ride 2 feet from the curb and feel quite secure. But this time, I tried riding just 1 foot from the curb. Whereas traffic had given me a wide berth, now it often came within inches of my left arm. Believe me, while it may be disconcerting to have a car honk at you because you're in its path, it's much worse to have one whiz by so close.

Learn
from Others' Mistakes

Consider these three additional mishaps:
- Bob is riding slowly through a tunnel with his son in a child seat when they're struck from behind by a speeding car. Miraculously the child is unharmed, but Bob is seriously injured.

It's safer to ride about 2 feet to the left of the curb or shoulder because you're more visible to drivers.

- Sandy is cycling slowly on a limited-access road. As she rounds a curve a drunk driver hits her from behind.
- Dave brakes as a traffic light turns yellow. He is grazed by a car accelerating to beat the light.

Once again, these cyclists were within their legal rights. But each of the accidents could have been avoided had they acted more predictably and more like traffic.

The Safe Scenario

It's dangerous to ride slowly through a tunnel because drivers, whose eyesight may already be diminished by the reduced light, may have difficulty gauging the distance to a slow-moving bicycle. If Bob was unable to ride faster while in traffic, he should have been pushing his bike on the walkway.

Likewise, Sandy wasn't visible as she rounded that curve. Since she was riding slowly, the drunk had less time to react than if she had been pedaling rapidly. If she was unable to maintain 15 mph while in traffic, she should have been riding on the shoulder. Dave, too, was not acting like traffic, in that motorists might not anticipate a cyclist braking for a yellow light.

Wait, Like the Cars

One final point. There are few things more tempting to a cyclist than passing a row of vehicles stopped at a traffic light. This is one of the most dangerous things you can do. All it takes is one vengeful nut who resents having to brake for you again, and you might end up in the hospital. Remember: To be accepted as a part of traffic, you must behave like traffic.

▇7 CYCLING RULES FOR ANY ROAD

One of the most important aspects of bicycle commuting is safety. Today, more and more cyclists are hitting the road, so it's more important than ever to follow the rules—written and un-written—and use common sense.

No one knows this better than Sara J. Henry, a veteran cyclist and writer. She published her first cycling column in 1977, and she's been racing, touring, and commuting ever since. "When I worked as a sports writer in Washington state, I didn't even have a car. I went everywhere on my bike," she says. "I would bike 20 miles to get an interview. I'd park my bike around the corner and walk to the person's house or office." In this chapter, Henry gives us basic cycling rules for riding on any road.

Anything Goes

I was 16 when I discovered cycling. I was in love with a high school senior with long blond hair and a shiny 10-speed. He rode to my house every day that summer, parking his bike in the front hallway, using paper towels from my mother's kitchen to wipe away rivulets of sweat.

I bought a bike and learned to ride, fighting with the cheap derailleur and steep Tennessee hills. My blond senior went away to college in the fall, but I still had my bicycle.

I rode to school, sprinting like a demon, always dropping into French class a little late. I found other cyclists and rode with them after school and on weekends, cranking up the ridge to my home just as the sun was setting.

Then I discovered racing.

Safety Lessons Learned the Hard Way

Greg LeMond was still in grade school, and bike racing was strange and exotic. I won a few races, bought a better bike, and donned tight shorts, a bright jersey, and a "leather hairnet" (the leather-strap helmet predecessor to today's hardshells). My buddies and I zipped through traffic, whooshed down bike trails, and logged countless miles on lonely country roads. We sprinted on boulevards with our wheels a hair's-breadth apart and inhaled lungfuls of exhaust as we gleefully drafted trucks and city buses.

And we crashed—road rash, dented wheels, broken collarbones. Bike hits runner, dog hits bike, bike hits bike, car hits bike, bike hits car. You name it, we did it. One spring I broke a front fork across a dog's midriff and discovered the time-stands-still vividness of skidding down the road on my face, watching bits of gravel go by.

At 20, I landed on my helmetless, carefree head and fractured my skull. I turned 21 in a hospital bed, surrounded by family, friends, and birthday cake, with one heck of a shiner and a lump on my head I can still trace with my fingers.

Right then I began to think seriously about cycling. Maybe, just maybe, some of these accidents could have been avoided. During the next decade I went from touring, to commuting, to weekend rides, to triathlons, and along the way developed a set of rules that helped keep body and bicycle intact.

Respect the Automobile

One of the keys to arriving home unscathed is developing a healthy respect for the automobile. It is large, it is heavy, it is difficult to stop, and it can crush you and your bike in seconds. Plus, when you're commuting it won't be piloted by someone out for a pleasant Sunday cruise. The driver may be tired, daydreaming, angry—even drunk.

Look at yourself from the driver's point of view. He's seen you, he's passed you, and he's forgotten about you. But then you squeeze past a line of cars stuck in traffic and suddenly, you're in front of him again. He gets upset, mutters a few mild imprecations about cyclists, or leans on his horn.

For the sake of gaining a few feet, you've succeeded in turning one more motorist into another bicycle-hating driver. To protect yourself and the sport, behave in a predictable manner. Don't zip in and out of traffic. Don't run stoplights. Don't hop blithely onto and off sidewalks. Don't try to outsprint drivers. And don't ride on the wrong side of the road.

Always signal your intentions and remain alert. Be aware of what traffic is doing around you. Stare at the driver stopped at the next intersection and look for some clue as to when he might pull out. Listen for approaching cars as well. And always be prepared to take evasive action. If a car is heading toward you and there's no place to go, shout. Scream as loud as you can. Nothing else is as quick or as effective.

Stay Cool

Always stay cool. If a driver cuts you off, resist the urge to make an obscene gesture, shout profanities, or pound his car at the next stoplight. Don't do it, ever. You are dealing with a machine that can kill or maim you, and a driver who may even have a loaded gun in the cab.

In my more foolish days I once made a rude gesture at a truck that nearly hit me. But as the driver slammed on his brakes, a chill went through me. There I was, alone on a country road, facing a truck with two angry men inside. In the end nothing happened (they were taken aback when they saw I was a woman), but I learned a lesson. Take no chances. Make no assumptions. Just grit your teeth, smile, and wave. You won't risk inciting the vicious driver, and sometimes it will even embarrass the rude one. And once in a while, the driver may simply smile and wave back, making you realize this poor, vacuous soul had no idea he nearly hit you.

Coping with Canines

Dogs, dogs, dogs. The good thing is, you probably won't encounter many chasers on city streets. The bad thing is, even one can become a huge nuisance on a regular route.

You probably thought you'd envisioned all the terrible things that could happen between you and these slavering beasts, and then I introduce a new horror tale. Yes, I hit a mutt broadside at 20 mph, snapped my fork clean off, and flew along the road as the dog yelped away. (I do like to think it cured him of bike chasing, however.)

Although my bike was a brand notorious for faulty forks, there's no doubt that dogs remain a nuisance and a hazard. Speed, I believe, is the best way to deal with them. Give the animal as wide a berth as possible, then sprint like crazy. You'll probably outrun him if he doesn't abandon the chase at the boundary to his yard.

If the pursuit continues, yell "No!" or "Go home!" in an authoritative voice. At the very least it will usually break his stride. Next try the water bottle. Squirt him in the face and you'll gain a bit more time. Pump-swinging is also a possibility, but there's the risk of losing your balance or breaking your pump.

For dogs that are a continual nuisance, contact the owner or the local police. If all else fails, change your route. Unfair, yes, but we're talking survival here.

Heed Pedestrians and RR Tracks

Pedestrians can be nearly as hazardous as automobiles. High-risk areas include intersections, parks, and bike paths with bushes and blind spots. A friend of mine learned about the latter after a head-on crash with a runner that put both of them in the hospital.

Inanimate objects such as railroad tracks, sewer grates, and slots in wooden bridges also deserve notice. Skinny road tires, in particular, are prime candidates for catching in these things. And whenever your front wheel stops abruptly, the rear one is likely to keep going. Get the picture?

Railroad tracks are fairly easy to handle. Simply reduce speed and approach them at a right angle. Most sewer grates have openings perpendicular to the roadway, but some may still be angled dangerously. Watch for them. On wooden bridges it's often best to dismount and walk your bike. And never try to ride across a steel surface if it's wet. Also beware of painted road markings, especially when cornering in the rain.

Be Prepared
for Emergencies

There will be times when even your best plans fail. Be prepared. Carry identification and important telephone numbers so if the worst does happen, you won't be lying unconscious in an emergency room while your nearest and dearest worry.

If you're conscious and have been struck by a car that did not stop, memorize as much about the vehicle as possible and get the names of witnesses. Promptly report all accidents to the police.

But, remember, the best measure is prevention. Move like traffic, stay cool, and always respect the drivers

Part Three

INCLEMENT CONDITIONS

8 ■ RAINY-DAY RIDES

People in Seattle don't tan, they rust, the saying goes. Members of this city's active commuting community also know a thing or two about riding in the rain. You'd be hard pressed, for instance, to find another location where mudguards are so prevalent. Even racers use them. The same goes for breathable, waterproof fabrics such as Gore-Tex, which are worn as commonly as underwear by the general population. And when sealed bearings for hubs and cranksets became available, a great cry of celebration went up around Puget Sound.

Wet Road Safety

In fact, if you don't ride in the rain in Seattle, you don't ride. But commuters there have learned that wet weather needn't be unpleasant if you use the proper techniques and equipment.

Turning Corners

Corners are the biggest danger spots, whether you're commuting home through a downpour or racing on a rain-soaked criterium course. By keeping your bike as vertical as possible, you can avoid having the wheels slide sideways from under you. Of course, to reduce the angle of lean you have to take the turns at reduced speed. Many racers find that pedaling through rain-soaked corners aids stability, and it prevents them from leaning hard enough to risk a fall. The chance of a rear wheel skid can also be lessened by sitting far back on the saddle to keep weight over the rear wheel.

When traffic permits, try using a racer's trick and "straighten" the corner. To do this, approach the turn widely, gradually cut to the inside, then drift out as you emerge from the corner.

Climbing Hills

When climbing steep hills, and particularly when standing, your rear wheel may slip. Try using a lower gear while sitting, or shift your weight over the rear wheel when standing.

Braking in the Wet

Even the best brakes become less effective in wet weather. Typically, there's a delay as the pads wipe water from the rims. Sand or mud worsens this. Test your brakes early in the ride to remind yourself of the increased stopping distance that's required. Once squeegeed dry, the brakes may suddenly take hold, so be ready to loosen up a bit on the levers as soon as you feel the grab. During long descents, maintain a slight drag on the rims to keep them free of excess water and allow quicker stopping.

Apply the brakes before a corner rather than in it to prevent locking the wheels and sliding out. Always favor the rear brake in the rain because it's much easier to control a skidding rear wheel than a front one. Practice a rear-wheel skid on a straight-away to become accustomed to it.

Road Oil
and Other Slick Spots

Surface oil can also decrease traction. Use extra caution during the first few minutes of rain before the slippery accumulation has been washed away. Then the road will be much less slick, though still more than when dry. On a straight road, avoid the oil and make yourself visible to motorists by riding in their right-wheel track. And do as your mother told you and don't go in puddles. It's not uncommon to find a gaping hole underneath. Look behind for traffic, then steer around standing water.

Metal and painted surfaces are particularly hazardous when wet. Be wary of rain grates, manhole covers, steel plates over excavations, expansion joints, grated bridges, and all types of lane markings. Crossing railroad tracks at a right angle is smart anytime, but essential in the wet.

Tires and Traction

The two thumbnail-size patches that are your tires' contact points with the road grip remarkably well in dry, clean conditions. To increase their chance of doing the same on wet roads, one trick used by experienced cyclists is to reduce tire pressure about 6 to 8 psi, thus increasing the size of the contact patches.

Speaking of tire performance, when it comes to riding in the rain, not all models are created equal. In general, tires with softer rubber compounds provide a better bite in the wet, as do those with deep chevron tread patterns. Ask your bike shop for a model designed to channel water away from the contact patch. It should perform well in dry conditions, too.

Three Words of Wisdom

Smooth, steady, and a little slower are the key words to remember when cycling on roads slickened by sand, gravel, or wet leaves. The riding techniques for surviving on rain-drenched streets are equally useful when you encounter patches of these.

Of course, if you see gravel or sand ahead, the ideal solution is to steer around it. If that's not possible, get off and walk. But often such hazards appear suddenly in your path, before you can react. Then the best course of action is to do nothing. Braking suddenly or trying to steer out of gravel or sand will probably cause you to fishtail and fall. It's better to try to relax, steer straight ahead, and be ready to react if you feel yourself skidding sideways.

If you come upon a slick spot while entering a turn, try to keep your wheels straight as you pass over it. Confine your steering to just before and just after you cross the bad stretch. Stay off your brakes, which, of course, is always good advice when turning.

■9 HOW TO RIDE IN SNOW AND ICE

Commuting needn't be a seasonal activity just because you live closer to Minneapolis than to Malibu. Frigid weather and icy roads might make it impossible to ride every day, but with the right bike-handling skills and equipment, commuting is possible even when the mercury goes into hibernation.

Sharing a Snow-Covered Road

Sharing a snow-covered road with traffic sounds like a cyclist's nightmare, but it isn't. When conditions get bad, lots of drivers opt for public transportation or a day off. Those that brave the slippery roads drive slower and more alertly than they otherwise would. They aren't likely to take chances trying to edge by you when they can barely steer a straight line.

Provided the snow isn't more than a couple of inches deep, you can ride a road or hybrid bike. The narrow tires will cut through the unpacked snow to get a decent bite of asphalt. For even better traction, use tires with an aggressive, off-road tread. Several models are available for hybrid bikes and, depending on frame clearance, they may fit road bikes, too.

To ride through deeper fresh snow, or on roads packed hard by traffic, nothing works better than a mountain bike with the widest, knobbiest tires you can get. Run them at the lowest air pressure that prevents pinching the inner tubes—about 15 to 20 psi for most 2.125-inch or wider tires. Soft, fat knobbies have incredible traction on snow. They're much less likely than narrow tires to slip out from under you.

Slipping, Sliding, and Staying Upright

Clutching the handlebar in a white-knuckled death grip is the natural response when the rear wheel starts squirming through snow. But it's the wrong response. With fat, knobby tires, the bike isn't likely to slide out. Try to relax your upper body and allow the bike to seek the best traction. Keep pedaling smoothly—don't suddenly brake or accelerate—and you can plow through snow up to 6 inches deep for as long as your smoldering quads hold out.

For optimum traction on hills, don't use the ultra-low granny gears. They provide too much torque, which is likely to cause the rear wheel to break free with each pedal stroke.

Another secret is to avoid hard-packed ruts that grab your wheels and keep you from steering a path through soft, unbroken snow where traction is best. Once the snowplows have made a couple of passes and traffic has flattened the high spots, you can ride anywhere on the road, but use caution—hard-packed snow can be as slick as ice.

Fighting Invisible Road Hazards

Be alert for areas where there might be ice hidden underneath new snow. Metal grates, railroad tracks, and manhole covers also are especially slick with a dusting of snow. If you commute on the same roads regularly, you'll know where most of these hazards lie.

Sometimes you'll be caught by surprise on a slippery patch. Don't panic. Stay balanced over the bike, make no sudden movements, and let your momentum carry you past the danger. If you try to turn or swerve, the bike will slide out as soon as your weight is to one side of the wheels, dumping you hard. As long as you have momentum and are directly over the bike, you'll stay upright.

Even when roads are clear, be cautious when you are riding in below-freezing temperatures. Ice from snow melt, or the dreaded "black ice"—invisible frozen spray thrown on the road by passing cars—could be lurking around the next bend. Be suspicious of shady spots, because ice will linger there long after sunlit sections have melted and dried.

You may feel more comfortable cycling at 32°F than at 15°F, but snow and ice are slipperiest at the freezing point. If you can pack good snowballs, use extra caution. At colder temperatures, the snow is drier and provides better traction, so you can ride more confidently.

Weatherproofing Your Bike

Once you've got the bike-handling ability to stay upright on slippery winter roads, make sure your mount is up to the task.

Necessities

High on your shopping list should be a set of fenders. They're a convenience in a warm summer rain, but they're absolutely essential when the road is a sea of slush. They will stop much of the stuff from drenching your feet, legs and back, as well as the bike's drivetrain.

Your bike needs other protection, too. The chain is usually the first component to show the ravages of salt- and sand-laden snow melt, so keep it well oiled, adding more lubrication and wiping off the excess after every ride. If you lubricate your chain with paraffin or a heavy oil, it may skip in subfreezing temperatures. To remedy this, clean the chain in a solvent such as kerosene, dry it well, then relubricate with a light oil that won't harden and cause stiff links.

Also vulnerable are the inner workings of the hubs, pedals, and bottom bracket. If your bike doesn't have sealed bearings to keep out the nasties, slide rubber O-rings (available at a plumbing supply store) on the axles of these parts. (See chapter 17 for this procedure and other weatherproofing tips.)

Accessories

Because even the most skilled snow rider must occasionally put a foot down to regain balance, don't tighten toe straps while riding on slick roads. In fact, it's wise to use wide off-road pedals without straps. They'll provide a good grip with the heavy boots you may need for warmth and walking the bike through areas of deep snow or slush. If you insist on clips and straps, use pedals that provide a good grip on both sides. Then you can flip them over and ride clipless when the going gets tricky.

A winter commuting bike should also have a good headlight, taillight and reflectors, since dawn and dusk come much closer together at this time of year. Also, when choosing winter riding clothes, look for outerwear that has reflective stripes or panels. (For additional clothing advice, see chapter 18.)

10 SAFETY AT DAWN, DUSK, AND IN THE DARK

Are you commuting on a stealth bike? No, not one with a frame built of some high-tech composite that makes aircraft invisible to radar. Instead, we mean a bike that effectively evades more mundane wavelengths of the electromagnetic spectrum— specifically, those emitted by the headlights of cars hurtling toward you in the low light of dawn and dusk.

Safety Devices That Don't Clutter

Always remember: Just because it's light enough to see the road doesn't mean motorists can see you. Ideally, twilight riding requires the same safety accessories—a powerful headlight, taillight, assorted reflective doodads, and light-colored clothing— necessary for cycling in darkness. Problem is, most riders are loathe to burden their bikes with illuminative hardware that will only be useful at the beginning or end of an otherwise day-lit commute.

When you don't need full illumination, be creative and use reflective tape, reflectors, and small battery lights, combined with bright clothing. This will ensure your safety with minimal expense and clutter.

Safety Tape

If you ever driven past a cyclist who's properly prepared his bike for low-light conditions, the first things you'll notice are probably the pedal reflectors that are easily illuminated by your car's headlights. A simple safety measure. And it worked. You proceeded carefully and gave the rider plenty of room when you passed.

Pedal reflectors are a great idea. They're less obtrusive than the large spoke- and frame-mount types, and motorists can see them easily. But there are drawbacks: Most clipless pedals have no provision for a reflector attachment, and on traditional pedals they usually interfere with cleated shoes.

So how do you get the same benefits without the drawback? Reflective tape. Strips of Scotchlite or a similar product applied to your bike's pedals, front and back of crankarms, or even the heels of your shoes will grab the attention of approaching drivers. The same tape, stuck discreetly to strategic spots on the bike frame, will help define its shape for approaching motorists.

Short pieces of reflective tape, stuck on rims between spoke holes, become rotating beacons in headlight glare. These are available at bike shops, as are other forms that attach to the spokes. Tires with reflective sidewalls, common in Europe, are effective in defining a bicycle to a car approaching from the side. These are becoming more widely available in North America.

Reflective Clothing

Your helmet should be light-colored and bear a reflective cover or tape. Likewise, make sure your jersey or jacket is visible by choosing white or a light hue, preferably with reflective Scotchlite piping. You can also purchase a lightweight mesh vest with reflective strips. Even the humble seatbag can be a safety beacon, as these, too, are available with reflective patches.

Battery Lights

To supplement a reflectorized bike and body, consider using small, easily detached battery lights. And just as moving reflectors on pedals are noticed first, moving or blinking lights attract more attention than steady, static beams.

Here are several effective lighting accessories you'll want to consider for maximum safety. (See the photo on the opposite page.) These are good insurance if an approaching car doesn't have its lights on (which would otherwise activate your reflectors). Prices listed are approximate.

The water-resistant Cateye halogen headlamp ($20) attaches easily to any handlebar. Including the mounting bracket and two C-size batteries, it weighs just 113 grams. It's mostly an emergency item or attention grabber for motorists in murky light because it illuminates only a short section of roadway.

The Bike Nashbar Strobe ($17) can quickly be strapped to your arm or leg. It flashes every second and runs for about 15 hours on a C-size battery.

A variety of lights is available for night riding, including: the Cateye hal
ogen headlamp(top left), Belt Beacon (top center), Whee Light (top right),
Bike Nashbar Strobe (center left), VistaLite (center right), and BodyLight
(bottom).

The blinking Belt Beacon ($22) utilizes the same lamp as
a highway barrier signal. Its 60 flashes per minute are visible from
a mile away. It's also waterproof and convenient to use, clipping
onto a jersey pocket. An alkaline 9-volt battery lasts up to 140
hours.

The VistaLite ($15) mounts on a bike's rear reflector bracket or rack. Its red light-emitting diodes pulse six times a second and never need replacing. The unit will operate for more than 300 hours on two AA-size alkaline batteries. The weatherproof prismatic lens also doubles as a rear reflector. A model that sells for $17 features a clip for quick attachment to a rear pocket or belt.

The Whee Light ($35), although it's coiled around itself in the photo on page 53, should be strung through the spokes for increased side visibility—great for routes with lots of cross traffic. The plastic tubing houses eight tiny lights that are more visible than a normal reflector. The 8.3-ounce battery pack fits around the hub. It contains four AA-size batteries and will operate for 3 to 4 hours on a charge (recharger included).

The BodyLight ($70) belts around the waist. A 6- by 1-inch strip glows incandescent blue, which is especially effective at twilight. However, the 9-volt battery is exposed, and its weight can make one side droop. While this doesn't affect performance even in wet conditions, it does detract from the unit's appearance.

Rechargeable Lighting Systems

In recent years, bicycle lighting systems have undergone a revolution, thanks mostly to American inventors. They've succeeded in designing powerful, long-lasting, simple-to-use, rechargeable systems for commuters and other serious riders who ride in full darkness.

Such lights are more expensive than those with throw-away batteries, which may suffice for occasional use. But for a commuter who faces one or two rides per day in the dark, these systems become a bargain. Besides the ability to recharge the battery, they offer superior performance and reliability. Prices range from around $50 to $200 for models such as the Nightsun, Brite Lite, Cycle Ops, Nice Lite, Supernova, Velo-Lux, and Esge-IKU.

Choosing the Right Light

When shopping, you'll find a range of styles, mounting positions, and features. But for most riders, the most important consideration is which of two types of batteries—lead acid gel cell or nickel cadmium—a system uses. Each delivers good performance, so the choice should depend on your needs. Here are the guidelines.

Gel cells are the same type used in cars. They are the less expensive type in case you need to replace one, but they require more care. They must not be drained, which reduces their life, so the light should be switched off before it yellows. For maximum life you must keep them charged or stored in a refrigerator when not in use.

Nickel cadmium batteries thrive on "deep cycling" (exhausting and then recharging). You can't ruin them through overuse, so they have a longer lifespan than gel cells. They are also smaller and lighter. (Gel cells are usually oversize to keep you from discharging and damaging them.) Their disadvantage is that they lose power rapidly at the end of their charge, so you can find yourself abruptly without light if you ride too long. Gel cells fade more gradually.

On average, either type of battery will provide 3 hours of light when fully charged. Recharging typically takes about 12 hours.

Beam shape is also important. Ideally, it should be long and wide. The latter is necessary to fill corners with light, while the former allows safer fast riding, such as when going downhill. It's nerve-wracking to be riding on the edge of the light, fearing a surprise from the darkness ahead. In *Bicycling* magazine tests, the dual-beam Nightsun Team Issue ($195 with nickel cadmium battery) provided the most comfortable high-speed riding.

Most systems come with a taillight or offer it as an option. You can also use a separate battery-powered taillight that doesn't require wiring and won't drain power from the headlight's battery.

Part Four
NUTRITION AND HEALTH

11 NUTRITION GUIDE FOR EVERYDAY RIDERS

Bike commuting may not have the huge caloric requirements of racing or all-day touring, but it still requires attention to diet. Otherwise, incorrect food choices will lead to insufficient energy, making even a relatively short commute less enjoyable and causing you to drag on the job. But eat right and the opposite will happen. Commuting will be invigorating, and it'll help you work better as well as control your weight and improve your health.

This chapter will bring you up to date with the latest thinking in cycling nutrition. If you've been bouncing from one food fad to another or are confused about how to eat better for greater health and energy, the following information will set you straight. It explains how to devise a diet that ensures the zip you need for commuting twice a day.

The Best Cycling Fuel

If you had a plate of pasta for every time you've heard the word carbohydrate in the last couple years, you could probably start your own Italian restaurant. There's a reason, however, why nutritionists hype carbo: It's your best fuel.

Essentially, carbohydrate is sugar. Simple carbohydrate is a single or double sugar molecule—usually glucose, fructose, galactose, sucrose, or lactose. These are found in nutritional foods (fruits, for instance) as well as less healthful fare, such as candy.

Complex carbohydrate is a long chain of simple sugars. It's often called a starch (potatoes and pasta, for example).

When you eat carbo, it's broken down and converted to blood glucose, the body's main fuel and the only type that can feed the brain. Glucose that's not immediately used for energy is stored in the muscles and liver as glycogen to be used later for fuel. If these storage spots are full, the glucose is converted to fat.

Carbohydrate is a better cycling fuel than protein or fat. Although stored protein can be converted to energy when glycogen and glucose become severely depleted, the process is inefficient. Stored fat can also be a fuel source, but it can't be converted to energy in the absence of glucose.

This is why you need carbohydrate. Not only does a high-fat/high-protein diet carry more calories and adverse health effects, it does a poorer job of providing energy for cycling.

Getting Enough
of the Right Stuff

During and immediately after a hard effort, simple and complex carbo are equally effective. But in your general diet, it's best to emphasize the complex type, which promotes significantly greater glycogen synthesis and offers vitamins, minerals, and fiber along with the energy. Overall, nutritionists recommend that at least 65 percent of your calories come from carbohydrate.

Figuring Your Intake

Unfortunately, most food packages list carbohydrate in grams rather than percentage of calories. This makes determining your intake difficult. To help, follow these two steps:

1. First, determine your total caloric requirement by multiplying your weight by 15.
2. Now add 10 calories (for men) or 8 calories (for women) for each minute of cycling you do a day.

The total is roughly the number of daily calories you need to maintain your weight. (To lose weight, subtract 500 calories per day. You'll lose 1 pound a week.)

A 150-pound man who commutes by bike one hour per day would figure as follows: 150 × 15 = 2,250 calories + 600 calories (60 minutes × 10 calories) = 2,850 total calories.

For this rider, 65 percent of total calories would amount to about 1,850. This is the number of carbo calories he should eat daily. Since carbo has 4 calories per gram, he can divide 1,850 by 4 and determine that he needs about 460 grams of carbo a day. (2,850 total calories × 0.65 = 1,852.5 carbo calories divided by 4 = 463 grams of carbohydrate.)

Beyond the math, the point is that you should increase your intake of whole-grain breads, nonfat dairy products, cereals, crackers, pasta, rice, potatoes, vegetables, fruits, and juices. At the same time, decrease your intake of fat and protein foods, such as meat, cheese, whole dairy products (use nonfat varieties), and snack items.

Eating to Expand
Your Endurance

No matter how well trained you are, endurance is limited by one thing: the depletion of stored glycogen. When this happens, you feel light-headed, dizzy, and fatigued. You experience "the bonk." Fortunately, though, it is avoidable. There are ways to increase glycogen stores and prolong performance.

The best way is by cycling. As your muscles become better conditioned, they can store 20 to 50 percent more glycogen than untrained ones. To take advantage of this expanded capacity, you need to eat plenty of carbohydrate calories every day. Successive days of low intake can lead to fatigue and lackluster riding.

Drink to This

Besides a diet rich in carbohydrate foods, you can supplement your intake by using sports drinks or bars. These special products (available in most bike shops) are concentrated carbo sources designed to enter the bloodstream fast. They're ideal pre-ride foods and can even be used during a commute to keep your energy level high, particularly when extending the route for additional training.

To be effective, a sports drink should deliver about 40 to 60 grams of carbohydrate per hour. With most brands, you can accomplish this by drinking 1½ to 2 standard water bottles an hour.

For best results, avoid products with fructose (which is absorbed slowly). Look instead for sucrose, glucose, or glucose polymers. The last consists of several glucose molecules linked together. This chain is absorbed quickly, as if it were a single molecule. But in the bloodstream it breaks up, and you get the benefit of several glucose molecules instead of just one.

If you prefer to eat solid food, try energy bars or other high-carbohydrate selections such as bagels, bananas, or dried fruit. These are perfect on-the-job snacks during mid-morning or afternoon, giving you a quick energy boost while filling your fuel tank for the ride home. Unlike drinks, these foods do not enhance hydration. So drink plenty of water with them.

A Matter of Fat

Next to carbohydrate, fat is your body's best fuel. It's primarily useful on long, slow rides, when your intensity is low. But don't assume this gives you license to eat all the ice cream and french fries you want. We all have plenty of stored fat and, in fact, most of us have too much. While we can store only limited amounts of glycogen, we can stockpile unlimited fat, which can be burned only in the presence of glucose. For this reason, what we need is carbohydrate, not more fat.

This isn't to say body fat is useless. It does store vitamins and provide insulation. But in excess, it's one of the biggest health risks imaginable. It increases susceptibility to heart disease, high blood pressure, certain cancers, and diabetes.

Any kind of food can turn into body fat if you eat too much. But not surprisingly, the most likely source for body fat is dietary fat. Compared to protein and carbohydrate, dietary fat has more than twice the calories (9 instead of 4 per gram) and appears to be stored more readily.

For optimal health and performance, nutritionists recommend that you derive no more than 30 percent of your total calories from fat, and no more than 10 percent from the saturated fats found primarily in animal products. The remainder should be the unsaturated form that comes from vegetable oils, nuts, and grains.

How to Trim Your Diet

One way to assure a low fat intake is to check nutrition labels and select foods with less than three grams of fat per 100 calories. To be more specific and discover exactly what percentage of a particular food is fat, use this calculation: Check the product's nutrition label and multiply the grams of fat by nine. Then divide that number by the total calories in the food. The result is percentage of calories from fat. For example, one ounce of Velveeta Process Cheese Spread has 80 calories and 6 grams of fat. The calculation is: 6 (grams of fat) × 9 (calories per gram of fat) = 54 fat calories. Fifty-four divided by 80 (total calories) = 67.5 percent of calories from fat. (To figure a food's percentage of calories from carbohydrate or protein, multiply the number of grams of that nutrient by four instead of nine, then divide by total calories.)

You can trim fat from your diet by reducing your intake of animal foods. When you do consume them, select lean cuts of meat, skinless poultry, and nonfat dairy products. Also, cut down on butter and margarine, salad dressings, and hydrogenated and tropical oils, which are prevalent in many baked goods.

Interestingly, the fitter you are, the quicker you'll burn fat. A well-trained body is capable of bringing more oxygen into the muscles, thus increasing the rate of fat metabolism and sparing some glycogen stores.

Protein: Enough Already

Cyclists require more protein than sedentary people. But this doesn't mean you have to increase your protein intake. In fact, you're probably already getting more than you need.

One reason cyclists need extra protein is for fuel. Once muscles have depleted their primary source (carbohydrate), they begin using protein, according to new studies.

"Protein can be a small but significant source of energy — about 5 to 10 percent of total energy needs," says Michael J. Zackin, Ph.D, of the University of Massachusetts Medical School. "Protein calories become increasingly important in carbohydrate-depleted states. If you ride more than an hour a day and begin to deplete glycogen stores, you become increasingly dependent on body protein for energy."

The Recommended
Daily Allowance

Though results vary widely, Dr. Zackin says cycling may raise your protein requirements 20 to 90 percent beyond U.S. Recommended Daily Allowances. (The USRDA is 0.363 grams of protein per pound of body weight. For a 150-pound man, this is about 54 grams a day; for a 120-pound woman, about 43 grams. Add the 20 to 90 percent, and the male cyclist's daily protein intake rises to 65 to 103 grams, the woman's to 52 to 82 grams.)

But most active people are already at these levels or beyond. This was illustrated in a recent study of eight highly trained women cyclists. Although their diets fell short of recommended values for many nutrients, their protein intake was 145 percent of the USRDA.

High protein levels aren't hard to reach. For instance, three ounces of meat, fish, or poultry contain 21 grams. A cup of beans has 14 grams, 3 tablespoons of peanut butter have 12, and a cup of nonfat milk contains 9. All this adds up quickly. In fact, the average American consumes 100 grams a day.

The Best Sources

So unless you're a strict vegetarian or a chronic dieter, don't worry about increasing your protein intake. Instead, worry about where your protein comes from. The best sources are low in fat and include a healthy dose of complex carbohydrate. Muscles are built by work, not extra protein, and work is best fueled by carbohydrate.

Some low-fat, high-protein choices include whole grains, beans, vegetables, fish, skinless poultry, soy products, lean cuts of meat, and nonfat dairy products. Even vegetarians can get plenty of high-quality protein with a varied diet combining grains, legumes, nuts, seeds, vegetables, dairy products, and eggs.

Overall, nutritionists say 15 percent of your diet should be protein calories. But don't sweat it. This is one nutrition goal you'll reach without even trying.

▪ 12 BEST BREAKFASTS FOR COMMUTERS

Whether you're headed to work or a workout, your body needs fuel in the morning. For most cyclists, the breakfast of choice is cereal. In fact, Americans eat more than 20 billion bowls a year, and that may not be a bad idea.

The Benefits of Cereal

People who eat cereal have significantly lower fat and cholesterol intakes than those who consume other foods at breakfast, according to one study. Better yet, they have lower serum cholesterol levels than non-cereal-eaters and those who skip breakfast entirely.

What's more, a serving of cereal is inexpensive, quick to fix and clean up, low in calories, rich in important nutrients, and versatile, with dozens of varieties to choose from.

Some brands, of course, are little more than thinly disguised candy. But there are plenty more that provide top-notch nutrition. While any cereal is better than the typical bacon-and-eggs or pastry-and-coffee breakfast, the problem is determining which brands are best for a commuter's active lifestyle, especially since dozens of newcomers enter the market every year. The following guidelines should help you separate the best from the rest.

Remember that most data is based on a 1-ounce serving, which, depending on the cereal's density, may be more or less than you actually consume. As a cyclist with a big appetite, you probably eat more, so you may be getting double or even triple the calories and nutrients listed on the box.

Carbohydrate

One of the most important things you get from cereal is complex carbohydrate in the form of starch and fiber. Carbo is your body's most efficient fuel and should account for the bulk of your diet.

For morning commuters, cereal is a good choice because it digests faster than high-fat breakfasts, which means energy can be quickly delivered to exercising muscles. Most cyclists suffer no stomach distress eating a small bowl of cereal with nonfat milk (only about 200 calories) immediately before a normal commute. If you're taking a hilly route, however, you might want to allow at least an hour for digestion. Experiment to see what works for you. If you're lactose-intolerant (see the section titled "Lactose Intolerance" on page 68), avoid milk products before riding.

In addition, cereal can be a good snack to eat at work. Some cyclists even make Rice Krispies treats and munch them like energy bars, with pretty much the same positive effects on performance.

Fiber

Dietary fiber is vital for good health, yet most of us get only a fraction of the recommended 20 to 30 grams a day. There are two types of fiber: insoluble (which can't be dissolved in liquid) and soluble (which can). Insoluble fiber, found in wheat bran, can prevent constipation and can help protect against a host of bowel disorders, including cancer. Soluble fiber, found in oat, rice, and corn bran, can help stabilize blood sugar and, when eaten as part of a low-fat diet, reduce the risk of heart disease by lowering serum cholesterol.

Both kinds of fiber are a boon to the weight conscious because they help fill you up (and keep you full) with fewer calories. In fact, one study showed that subjects who ate a high-fiber cereal not only took in fewer calories at breakfast, but also ate less at lunch.

Getting the Most per Spoonful

But the type of grain you choose in a cereal (wheat, corn, oats, rice, barley, etc.) isn't as important as selecting a whole-grain product. Try to choose a brand that lists a whole grain as its first ingredient. These contain both the fiber-rich bran portion of the grain and the vitamin- and mineral-rich germ.

Some cereals offer one, but not the other. All-bran cereals have the highest fiber concentration (7 to 13 grams per ounce), but they lack the nutrient-rich germ and must rely on fortification. For extra fiber, a better idea may be to choose a whole-grain product with bran added, or top the cereal with fresh or dried fruit.

Virtually all processed cereals are fortified with vitamins, meaning they have a nutrient-rich coating sprayed on. In the production of these cereals, many important trace minerals may be lost, and these are not replaced. By selecting cereals whose first ingredient is a whole grain, you'll ensure that the nutrients are inherent to the food.

A Word on Selection

Select cereals with 15 to 20 grams of complex carbohydrate per serving and at least 5 grams of fiber. If the rest of your diet is short on fresh fruits, vegetables, grains, and legumes, consider a high-fiber cereal such as All-Bran With Extra Fiber (14 grams), Fiber One (13 grams), or 100% Bran, All-Bran, or Bran Buds (10 grams).

Fat

We all know the health benefits of avoiding fat. Fortunately with cereals, it's easy to do. Most manufacturers have made an effort to get rid of coconut oil and other fat sources. Some cereals are completely fat-free, including such old standards as Grape Nuts and Shredded Wheat. Most others contain 1 to 2 grams of fat, while a few (usually granolas and nut-rich varieties) go as high as 4 or 5 grams.

Choose cereals with less than 2 grams of fat per serving, and keep the fat content low by using nonfat milk.

Protein

Cereals contain little protein; usually no more than 5 grams per serving. This doesn't go a long way toward meeting the U.S. Recommended Daily Allowance (USRDA) of 44 to 56 grams a day, but most of us get more than enough at other meals. Besides, pouring on a cup of nonfat milk provides an additional 8 grams of protein to a bowl of cereal.

To get the biggest protein boost from cereal, choose whole-grain varieties. The protein value of any cereal can be increased by adding milk, nuts, wheat germ, etc.

Sugar

Sugar isn't the poison some people say it is. In fact, it's a good muscle fuel. Still, an overabundance in your cereal adds calories without nutrition.

While some "kiddie" cereals are as much as one-half sugar, most adult varieties are more sensible. Some, including Shredded Wheat, Cheerios, Toasty O's, Puffed Rice, Puffed Wheat, and many hot cereals have less than 1 gram of sugar. All-Bran With Extra Fiber and Fiber One contain no sugar but are sweetened with noncaloric Aspartame.

When reading labels, remember that 4 grams of sugar equal 1 teaspoon or 16 calories. If you don't sprinkle on more, that's an acceptable level. Cereals with dried fruit will have a higher sugar content, but that's okay because fruit is nutritious.

Unless a cereal contains fruit, its sugar content should be less than 5 grams per serving. Don't spoil a low-sugar cereal by applying too much. For a nutritional boost, sweeten cereal with fresh fruit or raisins.

Sodium

Salt can be problematic for people with hypertension, but compared with most processed foods, cereal doesn't have much. Some (including pure oat bran, regular oatmeal, Shredded Wheat, Puffed Rice, and Puffed Wheat) are sodium-free, while most of the rest provide 150 to 250 milligrams per serving.

There's no reason for a cereal to include salt, but a few brands contain more than even potato chips. Cheerios, Kellogg's Corn Flakes, Product 19, All-Bran, Wheaties, Chex, Total, Kix, Common Sense Oat Bran, Rice Krispies, and Quaker Instant Oatmeal are among those with more than 250 milligrams per serving.

(Most potato chip brands have 200 to 250 milligrams per ounce.) These salty cereals should be eaten in moderation if you're on a low-sodium diet. But generally, even if you eat two or three helpings, almost any cereal fits easily into a moderate sodium intake of 3,000 or 4,000 milligrams a day.

Choose cereals with less than 200 milligrams of sodium per serving if you eat large amounts.

Vitamins and Minerals

Virtually all cereals are enriched with vitamins and minerals, so don't be swayed by nutritional hype. Select a cereal that provides at least 25 percent of the USRDA for iron, but think twice about brands that supply 100 percent of the USRDA for all vitamins. You don't need a whole day's vitamins at breakfast, and these cereals are usually expensive. Any normal diet will provide sufficient nutrients.

Select cereals that provide about 25 percent of the USRDA for vitamins and minerals.

Your Cereal Checklist

Looking for an easy way to select a cereal? Check nutrition labels to find products that meet most or all of these guidelines.

- 15 to 20 grams of complex carbohydrate per serving.
- More than 5 grams of fiber per serving.
- Less than 2 grams of fat per serving.
- Less than 5 grams of sugar per serving (unless dried fruit is a major ingredient).
- Less than 200 milligrams of sodium.
- About 25 percent of the USRDA for vitamins and minerals.

Add Milk, Not Fat

Cereal is a high-carbohydrate, low-fat food, and to keep it that way it's recommended that you douse yours with nonfat (skim) milk. Here's how nonfat compares with other kinds of milk. The values in the table apply to 1 cup of milk.

Type	Calories	Calories from fat (%)	Cholesterol (mg)	Calcium (mg)	Protein (mg)
Whole (3.4% fat)	150	48	34	291	8
Low-Fat (2% fat)	120	38	18	297	8
Extra Light (1% fat)	100	27	10	300	8
Nonfat	85	0	4	302	8

Lactose Intolerance

If you're lactose-intolerant—unable to digest the sugar (lactose) in milk—you may find yourself avoiding cereal because the milk causes cramps, bloating, gas, and diarrhea. Lactose intolerance is prevalent among some races (notably blacks and Asians). In addition, most of us produce less lactase (the enzyme that breaks down lactose) as we age.

To counteract the problem, you can use a lactase-containing milk such as LactAid. It comes in nonfat and low-fat varieties that carry the same nutritional value as regular milk. And because fermentation breaks down lactose, those who can't tolerate milk may have no problem when mixing cereal into yogurt or topping it with kefir or sweet acidophilus milk.

Soy milk (available in health food stores) is also an effective option, as is a product called Vitamite, which apppears in most supermarket dairy cases. A nondairy milk substitute made with corn syrup, vegetable oil, and soy protein, it contains more fat than 2 percent milk, but it's almost entirely unsaturated, and there is no cholesterol or lactose.

Other possibilities for lactose-intolerants are moistening cereal with fruit juice or purchasing milk digestant tablets or drops from a pharmacy or health food store.

▄**13**▄ CYCLING WITH A COLD

Under the weather, they call it. Your throat is sore, your nose is runny. Your voice is beginning to take on an identity of its own. You've been blessed ten times today, and you weren't even in church. Tomorrow you have to be at work, though, and there's no sense trying to commute by bike because it'll only make things worse. Or will it?

The common cold is aptly named. At any given time, 12 million Americans are coughing, sneezing, and generally feeling lousy due to a cold. Though the symptoms are seldom serious, it costs us 30 million work and school days annually.

The Attack of 200 Viruses

During winter, many cyclists blame the damp, cold weather they ride in. But actually, colds have nothing to do with climate. Benjamin Franklin first said it two centuries ago, and numerous researchers have supported his claims. In some studies, near-naked subjects have stood in drafty hallways or freezers for two hours without increasing susceptibility.

"In all likelihood, we get colds more frequently in winter because more people are indoors," says Elliot C. Dick, Ph.D., a professor of preventive medicine at the University of Wisconsin. Children are more susceptible to colds than adults because they haven't developed as many antibodies. They acquire cold germs in school and day care and take them home to their parents, who spread them at the office.

"We refer to the common cold as if it were a single illness," says Dr. Dick, "but there are actually 200 viruses that cause the symptoms." Against these odds, it's not surprising that colds occur. But what's important is knowing how to respond when you get one. Some cyclists try to ride through it, hoping their fitness has made them strong enough to defeat the virus. Others, heeding the advice of mothers everywhere, rest at the first symptom. Either choice can be correct, depending on the situation.

To Ride, or Not to Ride

Unfortunately, there is no clear answer as to when cycling (or any exercise) is beneficial and when it's detrimental. In fact, the topic is a source of debate among exercise physiologists. They do agree on one thing, however: It's important to determine whether you have a cold or something more or less severe.

Generally, a cold causes a runny or stuffy nose, sneezing, and a sore throat. If the discharge from your nose is colored, and your symptoms are mild and confined to the upper respiratory tract (nose and throat), it's only a cold. But sometimes more serious complications can result, including middle ear infection, pneumonia, and in rare cases, heart complications and even death. Usually, however, a cold disappears within two weeks.

If your nasal discharge is clear, it's likely from an allergy, such as hay fever. If you have a fever, headache, severe dry cough, and aches and pains, you probably have the flu. In this case, physiologists agree, your bike should be off limits.

A Case for Riding

If you have a cold, cycling may be just what you need, according to at least one expert. Harvey B. Simon, M.D., assistant professor of medicine at Harvard Medical School, says exercising with more serious infections is ill advised, but working out with a cold is a good idea.

"If anything, anecdotal evidence says that some athletes feel better exercising with colds," he says. "This would make sense because exercise can increase mucus flow, which might provide relief for upper respiratory tract symptoms."

A Case for Not Riding

Other experts disagree, however, advising rest until the symptoms fade. One reason is that it's impossible to know how serious the symptoms are—especially in the first few days. If the virus has affected the heart, exercise can be fatal. But even if it doesn't kill you, the stress of riding can turn a minor cold into something worse.

"If you decide to wage a battle on two fronts—cycling on one end and fighting a viral infection on the other—your body may say, 'I'm being overwhelmed, so I may have to give you a case of walking pneumonia to get you out of the saddle,'" says Bryant Stamford, Ph.D., director of the Health Promotion Center at the University of Louisville.

Riding and Cold Remedies

Many commuters will be tempted to simply take a cold remedy and keep riding. This can be problematic, however, since most over-the-counter cures provide little relief and others don't mix well with exercise.

For instance, antihistamines are virtually useless against colds and can cause drowsiness. Similarly, vitamin C has limited value, though large doses (2,000 milligrams a day) may alleviate some symptoms. Decongestants do help eliminate a runny nose and pose no side effects for exercise. But aspirin and ibuprofen can be risky. By masking aches and other symptoms, they create the illusion that there is no virus. You're likely to ride as usual, which can make things worse.

Commuting Guidelines

The wisest advice is somewhere between these extremes. You may not need to stop riding to work for two weeks or more, as some experts would urge. Nor should you ignore the message your body is sending.

A Doctor's Advice

Edward R. Eichner, M.D., professor of medicine and chief of hematology at the University of Oklahoma, offers these guidelines:

- Ride if symptoms are above the neck (i.e., runny nose, scratchy throat, sneezing). But keep your intensity low, and cease cycling if discomfort increases.

How to Stay Healthy

The average person gets two to six colds a year, but don't think coughs and sniffles are inevitable. In fact, there are several ways to lower your susceptibility. And one of them is cycling.

Research by David C. Nieman, D.H.Sc., suggests that a moderate training schedule can help prevent colds. During a 15-week study at Loma Linda University in California, Dr. Nieman examined the cold-fighting abilities of sedentary women and those walking 45 minutes a day, five days a week. The walkers still got colds, but their viruses lasted half as long as the control group's. Thus, being fit can reduce the length of your cold. In addition, the active group's natural killer cell activity increased by 20 percent. (Natural killer cells attack cold viruses.)

Nevertheless, a moderate training program isn't the only way to avoid colds. Try these tips.

Don't share water bottles. Researchers at the Centers for Disease Control say enteroviruses (one of many viruses responsible for the common cold) can spread this way—though they're not sure if the water or the nozzle harbors the virus.

Get plenty of rest and eat a well-balanced diet. This may sound like something Marcus Welby would say, but it's still good advice. Both factors are instrumental in keeping the immune system strong.

Use disposable tissues. Forget handkerchiefs. Viruses live on them and can spread to bystanders every time you take it out of your pocket.

Avoid people with colds. Personal contact is the most common way to catch a cold.

Relax. Stress can weaken the immune system, according to studies at England's Common Cold Research Unit. Conversely, studies also show that happy, upbeat people with lots of friends are more likely to stay healthy (as long as their friends don't have colds).

Keep your hands clean. Colds are often spread by touching an infected person, then wiping your eyes or nose with infected fingers.

Inherit good genes. Although it doesn't seem fair, 5 percent of the population never get colds.

- Don't exercise if you have full-body symptoms (fever, loss of appetite, or muscle aches).

In the end, caution should be your guide.

A Word on
Your Fitness Level

If your commuting is part of a cycling program aimed at greater goals, Dr. Stamford says a short amount of time off the bike won't hurt. "It's foolish to worry about losing a percentage of your fitness since it will be regained upon resumption of training." A week of inactivity, for instance, will cost you about 25 percent of the fitness you've developed. But it only takes two or three weeks to recoup. In fact, in some cases, the break might be just what your body needs. Soon after returning to action, some cyclists exhibit greater strength than before getting sick or injured. Greg LeMond and Davis Phinney are two pro racers who've come back better than ever after enforced layoffs.

Make the Ride
Short and Sweet

So take it easy. If you want to continue commuting, keep the route as short and easy as possible. It might clear your stuffed nose. But if you don't feel like it, don't try to be a hero. Your mother was right—the rest will do you good.

14 THE EFFECTS OF AIR POLLUTION

It's warm, but not hot—a beautiful day for taking your long route to work. The sky is clear and the wind calm. But while finishing breakfast, you hear a radio bulletin warning of a Stage 1 smog alert.

Undaunted, you decide to do the 25-miler anyway. But by the end you're experiencing shortness of breath, you're beginning to cough, and a headache is coming on. The route bypassed several factories and a six-lane highway, and you noticed the air seemed heavy. At the finish, your time was significantly slower than normal, and several other commuters at work said they were experiencing similar symptoms.

What happened is not unusual among cyclists who ride in metropolitan areas, especially during the summer. Every day thousands of tons of organic gases, oxides, and particulates are released into the atmosphere, and they can adversely affect your performance.

The Dangers of Ozone

One of the major components of smog is ozone. It's produced photochemically via the action of ultraviolet radiation on unburned gasoline vapors and other gases. While ozone in the upper atmosphere is essential for life, ozone in the lower atmosphere is dangerous, impeding breathing and irritating the upper respiratory tract and eyes. Once created, it remains trapped until a major weather front clears the air.

Warm-Weather Cities

The problem is especially acute in warm-weather cities. For example, in late summer and early fall Los Angeles frequently exceeds the 0.12 parts per million (ppm) standard deemed safe by the Environmental Protection Agency. In fact, Southern California has an air quality agency that monitors ozone levels. It considers 0.20 a Stage 1 alert, 0.35 a Stage 2 alert, and 0.50 a Stage 3 alert. Although it's rare for L.A.'s air to reach the Stage 2 level, some of the area's reporting stations reach Stage 1 almost 40 times a year.

Ozone pollution is also a problem for cyclists in the Sunbelt. However, in more seasonal climes, such as the Northeast and Midwest, it's virtually nonexistent. Instead, carbon monoxide and other industrial pollutants are more prevalent.

Effects on the Body

Research confirms that a Stage 1 smog alert reduces the body's capacity for exercise. In a study conducted at the UCLA School of Medicine, 17 road cyclists were exposed to varying levels of ozone (0.00, 0.12, and 0.20 ppm) while riding stationary bicycles for 60 minutes in an 80°F chamber. Their breathing and ability to maintain a high cadence were significantly impaired at the Stage 1 level. In this atmosphere, the researchers concluded, riding may not be worth the risk, since significant discomfort and short-term damage may occur. The riders in the study were not appreciably affected by lower levels of ozone, although they did experience some temporary lung impairment and mild discomfort. Thus, the threshold for a significant reduction in performance appears to be between 0.12 and 0.20 ppm of ozone.

Research during the mid-1970s also showed that high ozone concentrations inhibit performance. Subjects engaged in strenuous exercise after being exposed to conditions simulating an average-to-bad air quality day in Los Angeles. After just 1 hour of exposure, they couldn't complete a 60-minute exercise test. Many complained of chest pain, nausea, headache, and shortness of breath. In actual conditions, the effects could be worse because of heat and other pollutants.

Can the Body Adapt?

If conditions are this bad, you're probably wondering how residents of L.A. and other major southern and southwestern cities exercise on a daily basis. Well, it's also been shown that the body adapts to continued exposure to ozone. As yet, physiologists don't know if this is a healthy adaptation similar to the body's response to altitude and heat, or whether it's destructive at the cellular level and injurious over the long term. It may well be the latter. Adaptation only suggests that there is less constriction of the air passages, which means the ozone may be able to penetrate deeper into the lungs and cause more damage.

Avoiding the Dangers of Ozone

If true, such a situation presents a dilemma for those who ride in smoggy cities. Do you forgo commuting, or risk possible long-term health problems? One solution is to ride before the morning rush hour when ozone levels are low. At other times, pedal with a slow, steady effort. However, cyclists who are highly sensitive to ozone may have to stay off the bike when levels are moderate to high.

If posssible, use routes with low pollution potential during an ozone alert. Generally, ozone hazards are minimal during early spring, late fall and winter, so summer may be the only time you have to take precautions. Contrary to popular belief, surgical masks only filter out large particles such as dust. Next to a gas mask, there's nothing a cyclist can wear for pollution protection.

Carbon Monoxide Risks

The exhaust from motor vehicles comprises a variety of gases, solids, and chemicals, the major parts of which are carbon monoxide, hydrocarbons, and nitrogen and sulfur oxides. Carbon monoxide is the most familiar pollutant in exhaust and it, too, has a detrimental effect on cyclists.

It Reduces Oxygen in the Blood

Carbon monoxide combines with hemoglobin, the oxygen-carrying molecule in the blood, to form carboxy-hemoglobin. Carbon monoxide has a 200-times-greater affinity for hemoglobin than oxygen. By taking up binding sites in a molecule of hemoglobin, carbon monoxide impairs oxygen delivery to the blood, thus causing performance to decline.

When you're exposed to moderate levels of carbon monoxide (above 100 ppm), you might experience headache, nausea, decreased visual acuity, confusion, and slower reaction time. The national safety standard for carbon monoxide is 35 ppm (average) during 1 hour, which is sufficient to produce a blood carboxyhemoglobin concentration of 1.5 percent.

It Lowers
Performance Power

Two studies illustrate the detrimental effects of carbon monoxide on performance. In one, the carboxy-hemoglobin levels of non-smokers breathing 100 ppm of carbon monoxide while exercising at maximum on a treadmill rose from 1.7 percent to 3.9 percent in one hour. This resulted in a decrease in exercise time from 698 to 663 seconds.

The second study involved a group of swimmers who were driven around Los Angeles for an hour before a meet, while another group remained poolside. The swimmers who were not exposed to urban air performed much better.

While neither study involved cyclists, the results are still applicable. Carbon monoxide levels near heavily traveled roadways can negatively affect riding performance and comfort.

Traffic and Wind:
Other Significant Factors

Carbon monoxide levels in urban traffic can average more than 50 ppm, peaking at approximately 100 ppm at stop signals. These high levels may extend as far as 50 feet from the main stream of traffic. Even moderate traffic conditions can result in carbon monoxide levels of 30 ppm.

Wind speed and direction affect carbon monoxide concentration. For instance, a headwind or tailwind usually means higher carbon monoxide levels, while a crosswind tends to dissipate much of the pollution. Riding along the upwind side of the road can significantly reduce exposure. Another factor is the presence of trees, tunnels, or other obstacles that trap polluted air near the ground.

Avoiding Carbon Monoxide

As with ozone, seasons of the year affect the concentration of this pollutant. Carbon monoxide levels are generally higher during winter for three reasons.

1. Cold engines produce higher concentrations of the gas.
2. The use of other fuels for heat add to the emissions.
3. The winds are lighter.

Carbon monoxide levels also vary with the time of day. In most cities the heaviest traffic occurs during the morning and evening rush hours. If possible, schedule your commuting rides so they don't coincide with the bulk of traffic, or at least choose the least-busy roads. And think twice before riding on those few days a year when your city is under a Stage 1 or higher smog alert.

Part Five
BIKE CARE AND EQUIPMENT

15 CONVERTING YOUR BIKE FOR COMMUTING

One of the first questions a prospective commuter asks is, "Do I need to buy a special bike?" Probably not. Although it's convenient to have a model with low gears and the clearances, eyelets, and braze-ons that allow easy installation of mudguards (fenders) and racks, almost any bike can be modified to work well for commuting. Even better, in most cases the conversion can be made for less than $100.

If your prospective commuter is a mountain bike or a road model designed for touring, you're in luck. It's very likely that all you'll have to do is buy and install the tires and accessories you want. There will be eyelets for racks and mudguards on the front and rear dropouts, and possibly even braze-ons for rack attachment on the seatstays above the rear brake. These models will also have the frame clearance necessary for installing virtually any tire that makes the bike better suited to city streets.

It's also possible to convert a road racing bike, but not without a bit more effort. Let's take a look at this "worst-case scenario," which includes problems you might encounter.

Converting a Road-Racing Bike

The main obstacle in turning a racer into a commuter is that it's ill-prepared for hauling. Regardless, it's even possible to convert one for long-distance touring if cargo is limited. The capacity should be plenty for most commuters.

Wheels

If the combined weight of your bolt-on accessories and carry-along gear won't exceed 10 pounds, lightweight 32-spoke racing wheels may be reliable enough. But for heavier loads or a city's typically rough, patched pavement, you'll have far fewer problems if you switch to 36-spoke wheels built with 430-gram or heavier clincher rims and install tires no narrower than 700 × 28C. Go up to 32C or 35C if your frame can accommodate them. (The clearance between tire and frame or mudguard should be at least ⅛ inch to allow for the wobble of an out-of-true wheel.) Choose Kevlar-belted tires for the ultimate in puncture resistance.

One way to avoid unnecessary expense is to purchase these beefier commuting tires (about $15 to $30 per pair) and try them with your present wheels. If all goes well, great. But if you suffer wheels going out of true, broken spokes or cracked rims, it's a signal to buy beefier wheels or have your hubs relaced with heavier spokes and rims.

Gearing

Most racing bikes have a 42-tooth inner chainring and a 24-tooth largest cog, yielding a 47-inch gear. This may seem low enough when you're climbing in the peloton, but on a hilly commute with a heavier bike after a long day on the job, you'll be wishing for less.

Since most racing cranksets won't accept chainrings with less than 42 or 39 teeth, the simplest way to get lower gears is to install larger freewheel cogs. A 32-tooth cog combined with a 42T chainring, for example, yields a 35-inch gear—adequate for moderate hills. A bike shop can supply cogs to fit your freewheel. They cost about $5 apiece.

You might find, however, that your rear derailleur doesn't have the capacity to handle such large cogs or the required chain wrap. If this is the case, replace it with a long-cage touring or mountain-bike derailleur. Many Japanese and European models are available, starting at $15. You'll also need a longer chain. Models such as the ever-popular Sedisport cost about $5.

If you can mount a 39T chainring and your rear derailleur will handle a 28T cog (most can), work up a 39/52T crankset with a 14–15–17–20–23–28T freewheel. This is possible with Shimano's popular 600EX, 105, or Dura-Ace racing groups. The capacities of Campagnolo's Triomphe, Victory, and C-record rear derailleurs vary, but the first two will accept chainrings as small as 35T and the latter will take a 39T.

If, however, you're stuck with a 42T chainring (this will happen with other Campagnolo and most SunTour cranksets) buy a new rear derailleur. Try a 42/52T with a 14–16–18–21–26–34T freewheel. If your frame has racing dropouts that limit the rear derailleur, go with 42/52T and 14–15–17–20–25–32T.

As another solution, you might be tempted to add a longer bottom bracket axle and install a triple crankset. Be aware, though, that on a racing frame with short chainstays, the extreme chain deflection will limit your use of the inner chainring to the largest cogs, and the big chainring to the smallest. Plus, you'll need a longer chain.

Once you've converted the wheels and gears, you've got the basis of a commuting bike. If brakes are worn, install quality pads, cables, and housings. Commuting conveniences such as padded bar tape, a wide saddle, and a rearview mirror are matters of personal preference.

Racks and Packs

Because of its short wheelbase, a racing frame won't be as stable as its touring counterpart when carrying a heavy load. Most commuters won't need to worry about this, however, except on rare occasions when weight exceeds 15 pounds. When it does, beware of a greater tendency for the front wheel to shimmy on descents.

A racing frame won't have dropout eyelets for attaching racks, so you'll have to buy special adapters (Blackburn makes them). You'll also have to attach seatstay rack clamps. If you want to use panniers, choose low-mount racks and bags for the front in order to center most of the weight at the axle. If you must carry a bulky item, put it atop your rear rack. If you're considering rear panniers, they'll probably need to be relatively small because a racing bike's short chainstays limit heel clearance. If you don't require so much capacity, consider a large, wedge-shaped, under-the-seat bag. This is a better choice than a handlebar bag, which could destabilize a steep-angle racing frame.

Mudguards

When purchasing mudguards, make sure the front one is narrow enough to fit between the fork blades. Also check for clearance between the mudguard and tire at the front and rear brake. The rear wheel may need to be moved fully rearward in its dropouts to gain the necessary clearance behind the bottom bracket. Be aware that some racing frames may be too tight to permit mudguard installation without creative cutting and bending. Attach the struts to the dropouts with the same Blackburn-type adapters used for racks.

Modifying a Mountain Bike

For several reasons a mountain bike makes a great commuter. It comes with a wide gear range, including the low ones necessary for getting up hills without working up a sweat, and it provides an upright posture that helps you see and negotiate traffic hazards. Its durable frame, wheels, and components are a real advantage on rough city streets. Plus, it's unrivaled in load-carrying capacity.

Tires

A mountain bike requires certain modifications to make it suitable for the road, however. The easiest and most important is replacing the knobbies with smoother rubber. Tires such as Avocet's FasGrip City and Specialized's Fat Boy roll quietly and efficiently. For minimum rolling resistance, choose the narrowest width the condition of your streets allows.

Racks and Bags

As for carrying clothing and homework, a mountain bike's smaller and stronger wheels give you leeway in choosing a setup. Although low-mount racks and bags are always a good choice, there's the option of using conventional racks. Use any size panniers, depending on your needs. Unlike with a road racer, clearances won't be a concern. However, some mountain bikes designed for competition don't have dropout eyelets, so Blackburn-type adapters must be used.

Toe Clips and Straps

You might also want to install a set of toe clips and straps, or even substitute conventional road pedals. Outfitted in such a way, the mountain bike is well suited for commuting. Any extra weight from the wheels and frame is offset by the bike's durability and low gears.

16 BASIC BIKE CARE

A bicycle is easy to care for, since most of its parts are external. They're convenient to clean, lubricate, and adjust. This is fortunate for commuters who ride daily in all types of weather, because most mechanical problems can be avoided with just a little know-how and a few minutes of maintenance. In fact, when a bike malfunctions, it's usually due to one of the four mechanical problems detailed below. But before we get to the procedures for preventing and remedying each of them, there's something else that must be prevented—bike theft.

Deterring Thieves

It's estimated that each year, more than one million bicycles are stolen in the United States. If you'll be leaving your commuter bike where you can't keep an eye on it, it's cheap theft insurance to purchase a good-quality security device. Basically, there are two types: U-locks and cable locks. (See the photo on the opposite page and on page 88.)

U-locks

In general, U-locks are harder for a thief to defeat. They consist of a crossbar and U-shaped piece of steel. Most major manufacturers offer guarantees that will reimburse you for the price of your bike if it's stolen due to lock failure. However, these locks have some disadvantages. They are larger, heavier, and more expensive (as high as $60) than a simple cable and padlock. They're also comparatively difficult to use and less versatile because you must lock your bike to an object that fits within the shackle (usually a signpost, parking meter, or bike rack).

Cables

Cables are inexpensive (some as low as $8) and can be locked to almost anything (most are 6 feet long). Unlike U-locks, they don't require removing the front wheel, and because most are self-coiling, they fit easily in a seat pack or can hang from the seat rails. A key or combination padlock can be used, although some models have a lock built into the ends of the cable. However, a thief can cut most cables or break a padlock with relative ease. Thus, these are appropriate only for low-risk situations.

Of course, even the best lock won't save your bike unless it's used properly. Always secure the frame and both wheels, and examine the object you're locking them to. Ideally, it should be metal and not permit your bike to be lifted off. A thief won't hesitate to steal your bike and lock, then separate them later.

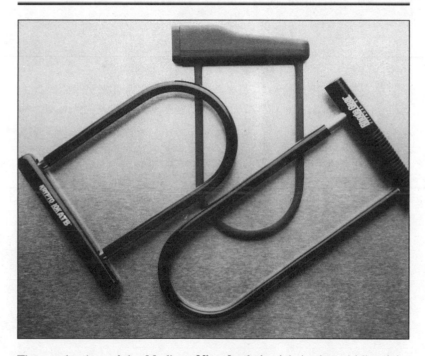

The mechanism of the Madison Ultra Lock (top) is in the middle of the crossbar to prevent prying. Kryptonite's KryptoLok ATB (left) is 5 inches wide to accommodate mountain bike tires. The Rhode Gear Citadel XL (right) is extra long and can be used to lock two bikes.

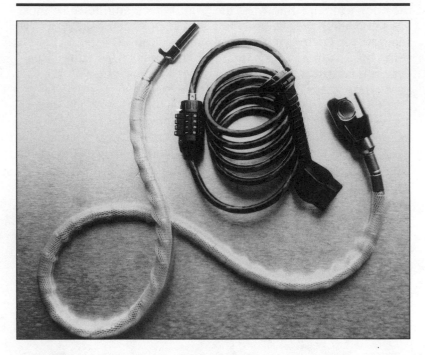

Cobralinks (left) is a high-security alternative to U-locks and consists of a series of links connected by ball joints. The Boa Cable Locker (right) attaches to the seatpost and easily holds a cable such as the Master Tough Stripes.

Preventing Damaged Tires

Pneumatic (air-filled) inner tubes and tires roll well, cushion the ride, and protect the rims from damage. But even perfectly good inner tubes gradually lose air through microscopic pores in the rubber. A high-quality butyl inner tube, for instance, can lose 30 percent of its pressure in a month.

Proper Inflation

Preventing underinflation problems such as poor tire performance, pinch flats, and damaged rims is simply a matter of inflating the tires to their recommended pressure (written on the tire's sidewall) once a week. Another good precaution is to squeeze each tire between your thumb and index finger before every ride to determine if they've lost pressure due to a slow leak.

Fat, low-pressure tires, such as those on mountain bikes, require filling less often. Once a month should do. But use the pinch test before each ride to check.

Knowing how to operate your tire valves will make proper inflation easier. There are two types of valves used on bicycle tires: presta and Schrader. Presta valves, also known as needle or French valves, are metal except for their seals. They can contain higher pressures than Schrader valves and are used mostly on high-performance road bike tubes. Before adding or releasing air, the top of the valve must be unscrewed and depressed momentarily. After the tire is filled, it must be tightened.

Schrader valves are the same as those on cars. But don't use a service station air pump to fill them. Such pumps are designed to fill high-volume tires quickly and can burst a bicycle tube.

Frame-fit and floor pumps for both types of valves are sold in bike shops. Some pumps have a reversible head and can fit either type of valve. Adapters that let a presta valve accept air from a Schrader pump are also available.

Quick-Release Hubs

Another part of the wheel that many riders neglect is the quick-release mechanism. Now found on most bikes, it's operated by the lever and hand-turned nut located at the front and rear hub. It's important because it secures the wheels to the frame. If it's open or loose, a serious crash can result. Quick-releases are used instead of bolts to allow wheel removal without tools.

Correct use of the front quick-release involves placing the wheel into the dropouts (ends of the fork) as far as it will go. Next, tighten the quick release by pushing the lever back until it's in the closed position. (Most levers are marked "open" and "closed.") The lever should rest in line with the fork blade or trail behind it. The squeezing force of the quick release can be adjusted by turning the nut opposite the lever. The lever should provide firm resistance as it is closed—enough to briefly imprint the palm of your hand. (Some bikes have fork dropout retainers that require unscrewing the quick-release nut several extra turns to remove the wheel.)

The procedure is the same for the rear wheel, except for the additional step of making sure the wheel is aligned with the seat tube (the frame member directly in front of the wheel). Also, indexed shifting systems work best when the axle is positioned near the front of the dropout slots. Before the quick-release is tightened, the rear wheel can be positioned fore and aft and centered. Many bikes assist this with small, built-in adjuster screws located at the rear of the dropouts.

If you're unfamiliar with quick-releases, practice using them and have an experienced cyclist check your work. While not a maintenance procedure per se, misusing them could result in crash damage that will require plenty of repair work.

Preventing Sticking and Grinding

There are plenty of moving parts on a bicycle, and most are exposed to road grit. Thus, they require lubrication to continue working properly. Bike shops sell a variety of spray and drip lubes.

Spray lubes usually come with a small plastic tube that attaches to the nozzle. This allows the spray to be directed where you want it. Drip lubes are even more precise. They come in small bottles and permit lube application one drop at a time. Many experienced cyclists favor the latter.

The Bike Chain

A commuter bike chain needs lubrication about once every 300 miles. A light coat is best because any excess will attract dirt and splash on the wheel and frame. To lube the chain, place the bike where you can freely turn the crank backwards. Put a rag over the lower part of the rear rim to keep it clean. Hold the nozzle near the chain, slowly spin the crank, and apply the lubricant where the chain passes over the top pulley of the rear derailleur. After you've done the entire chain, hold a lint-free rag loosely around it and turn the crank backward to wipe away excess lube and grit.

It's best to do this job 24 hours before riding. This will allow the lube's liquid carrier to fully evaporate and, thereby, keep things cleaner.

The Pivot Points

The pivot points—where moving parts meet—need occasional lubrication, too. The front and rear derailleur pivots are examples, as are brake arms and levers. (Don't get lube on the brake pads, though.) If these parts get dry and gritty they may stick. Spray or drip lube on each pivot and wipe off the excess with a rag.

The Cables and Housings

Modern cables and housings require less care than their predecessors, but an occasional squirt or drop of lube where each cable enters or exits a housing, and at the cable guides under the bottom bracket, will keep them sliding smoothly.

Preventing Loose Nuts and Bolts

Many problems are caused by a bolt or nut that worked loose or dropped off because of road vibration. This often happens to water bottle cages, racks, mudguards, toe clips, and other attachments likely to be found on a commuter bike.

Monthly Checkpoints

Check bolt and nut tightness at least once a month, or more often for a newly installed accessory. Use a set of Allen wrenches (available at bike shops) and metric wrenches to make sure each one is snug. Be sure to check:

- Handlebar and stem (6-mm Allen or adjustable wrench)
- Wheel nuts, if any (15-mm or adjustable wrench)
- Chainring bolts (5-mm Allen wrench)

- Crankarm bolts (screwdriver or 5-mm Allen wrench to remove dust cap; special 14- or 15-mm socket wrench for bolts)
- Accessories and hardware (screwdriver, adjustable wrenches, Allen wrenches)

Caution: Do not overtighten. Most nuts and bolts are small, so their threads can easily be damaged if force is used.

Preventing Cable-Related Problems

Cables will stretch until they reach a stable length. As this happens, the components they operate often come out of adjustment. For example, an indexed derailleur will shift poorly when its cable is loose. If you buy a new bike, your shop will readjust cables during a follow-up check (usually for free).

To help riders keep things working properly, manufacturers provide adjuster barrels. These are small threaded fittings on the brakes and rear derailleur that permit cable tension adjustment without tools. Turning them counterclockwise adds tension, tightening your brakes or taking slack out of the derailleur cable.

When your indexed rear derailleur doesn't shift as crisply as it once did, try turning its adjuster barrel counterclockwise one turn. If this doesn't help enough, try an additional half-turn. You'll know you've gone too far if shifts to smaller cogs become balky.

Finally, don't hesitate to ask your bike dealer for an explanation or demonstration of any aspect of basic bike maintenance. Most dealers pride themselves on service and will invest the time required to keep you happy. For more detailed procedures on all aspects of bike care see another book in this series, *Basic Maintenance and Repair,* and the "Repair Stand" department in each issue of *Bicycling* magazine.

■17 WEATHERPROOFING YOUR BIKE

Beyond regular lubrication, there are several ways to prevent the weather from ruining your bike. These tips are especially important when you're commuting, since your bike is more frequently exposed to wet and dirty conditions. Grit fouls the chain first, then works its way into the hubs, headset, and bottom bracket. Moisture can rust steel frame tubes inside and out. Here are some easy, inexpensive ways to prevent weather-induced damage.

Frame Protection

Handle your bike carefully to avoid chipping the paint. Don't lean it against the frame, and be careful when placing it on a car rack or in a trunk. If you do chip or scratch the paint, touch it up as soon as possible to prevent rust. If your bike shop doesn't carry paint, try an automotive store or hobby shop.

The Exterior

Wax the frame twice a year. Wax protects the finish against fine scratches and prevents rust. Car wax is acceptable, although framebuilders recommend using a soft, nonabrasive substance such as Bike Elixer Cleaner/Protector or Dave Moulton's Pro Frame Wax, especially for frames painted with lacquer. These two waxes do not leave a visible residue in hard-to-reach places, such as around lugs. (A Du Pont Imron finish does not need to be waxed, but it won't hurt.) If your bike is exposed to salt and moisture, whether from ocean breezes, winter road crews, or sweat, a lightweight lubricant such as WD-40 will help prevent corrosion if applied lightly to the outside of the frame.

The Interior

Whenever you overhaul a crankset or headset, or remove the seatpost, spray the inside of all accessible tubes with an anticorrosion solution such as LPS-3, available at hardware or auto supply stores. A light coating is all that's needed. You can also use oil, but it tends to flow to the bottom of the frame and evaporate.

Reducing Maintenance Time

Install mudguards to keep you and your bike much cleaner when riding on wet roads. They will significantly reduce the time you spend on washing and routine maintenance. Use full-size fenders—the more they cover, the better.

Chain Care

For frequently wet conditions, consider lubricating your bike's chain with a heavy oil, such as a foaming motorcycle chain lube, to repel water. Some road race team mechanics wipe a thin layer of white lithium grease over the lubed chain to keep moisture out.

Paraffin Treatment

Paraffin treatment is another alternative, particularly if you ride where it's sandy. It leaves the chain dry to the touch, so it doesn't hold grit or get grease on your hands or clothes. It also keeps the drivetrain pristine, eliminating routine cleaning. Here's how to do it.

1.   Use solvent to remove all oil and grease from the chain and the parts of the drivetrain it touches. Let the components dry.
2.   Soak the chain in a can of melted paraffin for at least 10 minutes. Very hot paraffin (300°F) penetrates best, but wax is flammable so don't heat with an open flame or exposed coils. A "Fry Daddy" or other electric deep fryer, placed outdoors where fumes can disperse, is handy for this procedure.
3.   Fish out the chain with needlenose pliers or a coat hanger and hang it so the hot wax can drip off. Allow the

chain to cool and then reinstall it. With your bike on a repair stand, spin through the gears to loosen the links and allow excess wax to flake off.

4. Repeat this procedure about every 300 miles or if the chain begins to squeak after getting wet. There is no need to use solvent for subsequent cleanings because the hot wax will flush away the grit. Replace the wax with new bars of paraffin (available at supermarkets) when it becomes dirty.

Preserving Bearings

To withstand wet riding conditions, pack your hub, pedal, bottom bracket, and headset bearings in a heavy, water-resistant grease such as Super Lube or Campagnolo's 02-ZPT. Some mountain bike enthusiasts advocate boat trailer wheelbearing grease, which is waterproof and available at marine stores.

Protect the Headset

Even if you use mudguards, headset bearings can be further protected with seals made from old inner tubes. It's convenient to install these during a headset overhaul. When the headset is apart, place 2-inch sections of inner tube over the top and bottom of the head tube. After the headset is reinstalled, pull the sections over the cups to seal out water and grit. They can be snipped off when no longer needed. (See the illustration on page 96.)

Seal Out Water
and Grit with O-Rings

Rubber gaskets known as O-rings are available from hardware and plumbing supply stores. Use them in a number of places to seal out water and grit. For instance, place them over the bottom bracket axle against the fixed cup and adjustable cup. Use several on each side so the innermost rings stay snug against the cups. (See the illustration on page 97.) Likewise, place O-rings over the hub locknuts against the dust caps and over the pedal axle against the pedal cage.

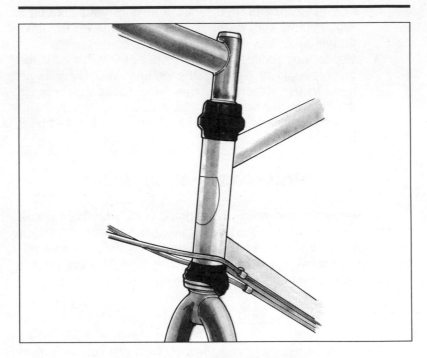

Use sections of old inner tube to protect the headset.

Other Weatherproofing Tips

Use the following tips to weatherproof your bike and keep it in tip-top shape:

- Remove and degrease derailleur and brake cables that run underneath the bottom bracket, then lubricate by running them through a cake of paraffin. The paraffin will not attract road sludge.
- Armor All keeps rubber brake hoods from drying and cracking. Don't use it on tires, however, because it makes them slippery when wet.
- If your bike gets immersed in water or caught in a down-pour, remove the seatpost (mark its position first) and hang the bike upside down to allow water to drain and

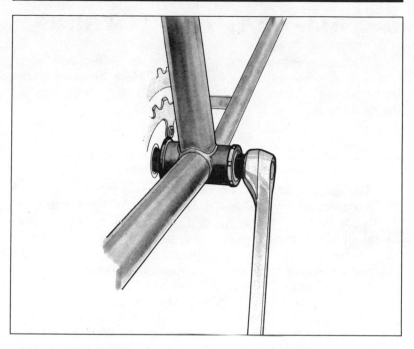

Rubber O-rings help prevent damage from water and grit.

tubes to dry. This isn't necessary for bikes that have cut-outs under the bottom bracket.

- In winter, consider parking your bike in a cool place to reduce the internal condensation that can occur when it's moved between warm and cold temperatures.
- If you have a saddle with a leather top, use a saddle cover on rainy days. If the leather gets wet, don't risk further damage by drying it too near a heat source. The same goes for other leather items, such as shoes.
- Take advantage of a rainy ride by using it to clean your bike. Since it's wet already, all you need to do it wipe off the water with an absorbent rag or paper towels. Then spritz the derailleur and brake pivot points with spray lube, and put some at each cable/housing junction. Add a little chain lube, wipe off the excess, and you're done.

18 ALL-WEATHER CLOTHING

Most prospective commuters have two questions about clothing: What's best to wear while riding? How can work clothes be transported? These are often presumed to be obstacles, but the answers are easy.

Pleasant Weather, Short Commute

The simplest solution is to ride in the same clothes you work in. This should be possible if your commute is short and the weather is pleasant. It also helps if your job allows you to wear casual clothes, although riding in a suit is certainly possible. It may not be as comfortable (or as practical when you find yourself in a sudden shower or needing to make a curbside repair), but numerous commuters do it. All you need to add is a helmet, gloves, and shoes that won't slip on your pedals.

Otherwise, use a fanny pack or bike pack to transport your work clothes each day, or use one day each week to drive in with a supply that you can store in the office. Combine this car commute with other errands that may be hard to accomplish by bike.

Double Duty for Your Recreational Attire

If you own recreational cycling clothes, you'll find them excellent for commuting, too. CoolMax and similar fabrics help control moisture for greater comfort in warm weather, and a brightly colored jersey will increase your safety in traffic. If you want to wear your cleated cycling shoes, buy rubber cleat covers so you can walk without slipping. Otherwise, invest in touring or mountain bike shoes that are stiff enough to resist pedal pressure but flexible enough for comfortable walking.

Clothes for a Conservative Style

Would you prefer a more conservative look? Casual wear designed for cycling is available through bike shops and mail order companies. You'll find jerseys with collars and shorts that have large pockets and a looser fit like those made for walking. But even though the appearance is conventional, the fabrics and comfort features are the same as those found in sleek-fitting cycling clothes. For instance, these so-called touring shorts contain a seamless liner inside the crotch to pad the saddle and reduce chafing.

Cold-Weather Gear

In chilly weather, a lightweight jacket with windproof front panels will keep you warm without overheating. Use the zipper to control ventilation. Underneath, wear a fabric such as wool or polyproplylene against your skin to wick dampness.

Protecting Your Legs and Torso

You won't need more torso protection even when the temperature drops into the 40s, but should it become necessary simply add another light layer. It is trapped air, not bulky insulation, that increases warmth best. A pair of cycling tights will keep your legs comfortable in chilly morning and evening air.

Protecting Your Extremities

Even on a short commute, your extremities can become painfully cold in winter temperatures. Protect your hands with full-finger gloves containing lightweight insulation such as Thinsulate. Cover your shoes with booties made of stretch Gore-Tex or neoprene. Wear a polypropylene balaclava over your neck, head, and ears. Most are thin enough to fit comfortably inside your helmet, which can be topped with a bright, reflective cover to improve safety and prevent wind from entering.

Rainy-Day Attire

Proper clothing can mean the difference between a pleasant (or at least tolerable) ride in the rain and a miserable slog.

Waterproof Jacket

One of the most essential elements is a good-quality water-proof jacket made of a fabric such as Gore-Tex, 3M Thintech, or Toray Entrant. Ideally, it should be a garment designed for cycling. This means it is cut to the shape of a bent-over rider, has an extended rain flap over the buttocks, provides ventilation, and is brightly colored or reflectorized with Scotchlite. It should also be compact enough to stow in your pack or under your seat. (Wrap it in a plastic bag and tie it in place with a toe strap.)

Extra Protection

Other items depend on the temperature. When it's cold, combine your rain jacket with one or two layers of polypropylene or wool on your upper body. It's important to have one of these wicking fabrics against your skin to help keep it from feeling wet and cold. For the same reason, wear wool or polypropylene tights and socks. The former will be especially effective if the legs have wind- and waterproof front panels. A cotton cap provides additional warmth, and the bill helps keep rain out of your eyes. (You should wear your helmet over the cap, so you may need to remove one or two of its pads.) Glasses can be prone to fogging and spotting, but they offer protection from dirt and debris thrown from passing vehicles and your own wheels. Clear lenses are best.

Of course, even with the best clothing, you can't stay warm and dry indefinitely. In fact, you'll find that you can get as wet from sweat as from rain, especially on a route with climbs. Use the jacket's front zipper to provide ventilation. Since you're in the riding position, not much rain can get through an opened jacket.

Reflective Wear

If you'll be commuting frequently in murky weather or darkness, consider buying some reflective clothing or accessories. Here are several examples of what's available. (See the photograph on the opposite page.) Prices may vary in your locale.

Bikealite's reflective helmet tape ($4 per roll) sticks securely to hardshells, thinshells, and Lycra covers. The $60 Bell Quest comes with a Lycra cover (also sold separately) that has a Scotchlite strip for high visibility.

Radioactive's jersey ($30) keeps you in sight with neon coloring for daytime visibility and reflective Scotchlite in the logo for nighttime attention.

The Bikealite cyclist's safety vest ($14) is cut longer in back than other models, so its reflective stripe can be seen better by motorists. Light and foldable, it's a good saddle bag emergency item.

The Scotchlite strips on Hind's Vision Short ($50) can be seen 2,000 feet away. They sweep from the rear to the sides of the short for optimum visibility.

The reflective panels on Nike's tights ($75) bob up and down as you pedal, alerting drivers of your presence.

For extra safety, illuminate yourself with Bikealite reflective helmet tape, a Radioactive jersey, a Bikealite safety vest, Hind Vision shorts, or Nike tights.

19 ACCESSORIES THAT MAKE COMMUTING CONVENIENT

While it's true that you can begin commuting with the cycling equipment you already own, there are many items sold by bike shops and mail-order companies that will make your rides safer and more convenient. This chapter provides examples of what's available. As commuting grows in popularity in the 1990s, it's certain that these and other companies will introduce more innovative products for the everyday, all-weather rider who needs to transport clothing, homework, and other items. Stay abreast of what's new and how well it works by reading *Bicycling's* New Products department. (The suggested retail prices will give you a general idea of cost, but they may be higher or lower at the time of your purchase.)

Bike Bags, a Must for Commuters

Inevitably, you'll end up carrying a lot of stuff while commuting. In fact, how to do it conveniently may well be a major concern. The solution is found in bags such as these. (See the photograph on the opposite page.)

Performance's Deluxe Handlebar Bag ($37) has an internal stiffener that will keep a brown-bag lunch from being crushed. Its front zippered pocket, two mesh side pockets, and nylon inside compartments afford plenty of storage space, and 3M Scotchlite reflective tape on the front enhances visibility. A clear plastic map holder on top will help you try new routes without going astray. A removable padded shoulder strap lets you carry the bag away after detaching it from the bracket that holds it on the bar.

The water-resistant Bike Nashbar Cyclist Attaché ($35) mounts securely to a standard front or rear rack. We found it works best on the former because, when hung from the rear, the heel of big-footed riders can strike it while pedaling. Inside, two large flap pockets hold files, and smaller compartments help organize your calculator, eyeglasses, pens, credit and business cards. The large-handle zippers won't rattle.

Cannondale's Expander panniers ($85 per set) easily attach to a standard front or rear rack. They zip out to nearly double in size, from 400 to 700 cubic inches. There are also two outer pockets and Scotchlite stripes for added visibility.

The Gregory Tail Wind fanny pack ($50) is a good choice for traveling light. The quick-release web belt holds the pack comfortably on the lower back, while a rubber mesh backing keeps it from slipping. The small size (shown in the photograph below) has a capacity of 288 cubic inches, while a larger model ($56) has 352. Both are water resistant.

Commuters can choose from several handy bags for transporting essentials. Clockwise from left are Performance's Deluxe Handlebar Bag, the Bike Nashbar Cyclist Attaché, Cannondale's Expander panniers, the Gregory Tail Wind fanny pack, and a Trek seat bag.

The Trek seat bag ($20) is brightly colored for visibility and can expand from 80 to 100 cubic inches to accommodate more tools, tubes, or a rain jacket. It's water resistant, and the quick-release straps are fully adjustable for secure cinching.

Convenient, Affordable Accessories

These affordable accessories will enhance commuting, saving your good humor, your bike, and maybe even your health. (See the photo on the opposite page.)

Zefal fenders ($20 to $30 per pair) are an inexpensive way to keep water and road grime in check. The lightweight plastic has an aluminum mesh core, so they're virtually indestructible and rattle-free. The fenders come in 35-, 44-, 55-, and 63-mm widths to fit most bikes, and four colors (silver, black, gray, white). They are guaranteed against breakage.

The Zefal Mini Pump ($8) is only 9½ inches long, making it easy to store in a fannypack or saddle bag. It converts for use on presta or Schrader valves. However, it did take us 398 strokes (almost 6 minutes) to fill a 26 × 1.95-inch tube to 45 psi.

The Silca Impero pump comes in seven colors and a variety of sizes to fit any frame. The pump itself is $10 and it accepts either a Silca ($3) or Campagnolo ($12) presta head. The model shown sports the latter, which, incidentally, is unsurpassed for bopping attacking dogs.

The Trek pump strap ($3.75) can secure just about anything on your bike. The 12½-inch-long strip of nylon has hook-and-loop fasteners for quick installation and removal.

Handlebar and helmet mirrors from Rhode Gear let you relax when the rear is clear. The handlebar mirror ($15) attaches to the brake hood via a belt with hook-and-loop fasteners. The helmet mirror ($11) is held in place with adhesive, and it has two ball-and-socket joints for full adjustability.

Kryptonite's K4 Lock ($35) comes with a $1,000 guarantee against theft (except in New York City). Known as a U-lock, this type is still the easiest and safest way to secure your bike. The K4 is vinyl-coated so it won't scratch your frame. Weight: 2.1 pounds.

The Life-Link bottle cover keeps liquid cooler longer. Simply soak it in water, slip it on a bottle, and start riding. Airflow over the cover prevents the contents from warming quickly. Available in two sizes: 20 ounce ($8) and 27 ounce ($10). In cold weather it can be used dry to serve as an insulator.

The compact Megahorn ($25) houses a piercing siren to warn pedestrians and surrounding traffic of your approach. The plastic, water-resistant unit straps to the handlebar and is activated by pushing a rubber button. It operates on a 9-volt battery.

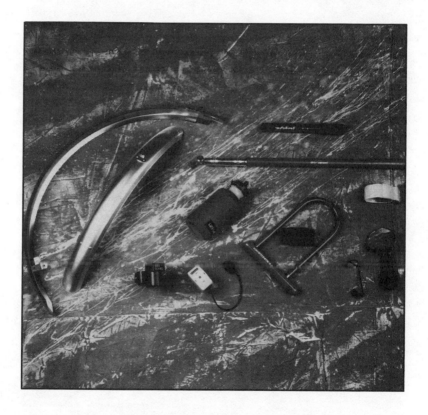

Shown here is an assortment of practical commuting accessories: Zefal fenders (far left), Zefal Mini and Silca Impero pumps (top), Life-Link bottle cover (center left), Kryptonite's K4 Lock (center), Trek pump strap (center right), Bike Guard alarm and Megahorn (bottom left), and Rhode Gear handlebar and helmet mirrors (bottom right).

The Bike Guard alarm ($20) is a nifty motion sensor that attaches under the saddle. It's triggered by even the slightest movement, and once activated will sound as long as the bike is moving. Its siren is loud, but the manufacturer recommends using it with a strong lock for added protection. The unit takes only about 30 seconds to install, and it's armed via a series of combination dials.

20 HOW TO FIX A FLAT IN 5 MINUTES

For most commuters, timing is everything. The morning schedule is calculated to get you to work just before the whistle blows, and in the afternoon you need to return home in time for chores or family obligations. There's usually little leeway for a problem that causes your commute to become longer than normal.

Proper maintenace will go a long way toward ensuring your bike's reliability, but there's one breakdown that can strike any rider at any time—a flat tire. It needn't cause a significant delay, however, if you can change tubes like a pro. In fact, the following procedure comes from one: Jim Langley, a *Bicycling* magazine editor who worked as a shop mechanic for nearly 20 years. In this chapter, Langley shares, step by step, his method that should put you on the road again within 5 minutes.

Pack the Right Materials

In your seat pack, carry a spare tube, two or three tire levers, a small rag, and, for insurance, a patch kit and some boot material (pieces of tire casing to cover large cuts). And of course, you'll need a frame-mount pump.

Some levers are better than others for certain tires. I usually don't use any, but when I do I prefer steel or aluminum models with thin ends for getting under tight beads. Plastic levers slide around rims nicely but have thick ends better suited to looser tires.

Parts Pointers

The quickest way to remove and install a tire is without tools. Most 26-inch tires are easy. However, 27-inch and 700C lightweight clinchers are different. With these, selecting the right tire, tube, and rim strip is key.

(Rims also affect removal, but unless you're about to purchase new wheels, you can't do much about this. If you are buying wheels, test the rims by installing the tires you'll use. I've found that Matrix ISO C and Mavic Open 4CD rims are easy to strip tires from.)

Choosing
the Right Rim Strips

Use the thinnest rim strip possible because thick ones increase rim diameter, making tire installation and removal more difficult. Exchange thick-rubber and rope models for cloth tape or polyurethane, making sure to use the correct width. Usually, narrow strips are for wide rims and vice versa. This sounds odd but it's true because the narrow rim has a wider well.

For a tire that's really tight even with a polyurethane strip, try filament packing tape. It's the thinnest solution and can easily be split lengthwise to fit different rim widths.

Finding
Easy-to-Remove Tires

Select easy-to-remove tires by testing different models on your rims. (See the section titled "Installing a Tire" on page 111.) For commuting, avoid ultranarrow tires because the tube completely fills them and makes them difficult to mount. Besides, they don't have the durability of wider tires. I recommend nothing narrower than 28C (1⅛-inch) tires for city streets, and these have plenty of room for a narrow tube. Tires are made with beads of stiff wire or foldable Kevlar. Once stretched, the latter type becomes easier to remove.

Using the Right Tube

Use a butyl tube that's one size smaller than the tire, such as a 700 × 25C with a 700 × 28C tire. However, you can't use this trick with polyurethane tubes, which don't expand and must match tire size. This makes them slightly more difficult to work with. Latex tubes, because they tend to be oversize, substantially slow tire changes.

To speed repair, you might want to try to leave off valve caps and nuts, although tubes with Schrader (automotive-type) valves should be capped to prevent grit from entering.

Removing the Tire

When people watch me replace a tube they often comment that I must have great hand strength. Actually, it has little to do with strength. It's my technique, not my muscles, that make it possible. Here's how it's done.

1. When you puncture a tire, stop as quickly as possible. If it's a rear flat, shift to the smallest freewheel cog while slowing. Get off, then open your brake quick-release or unhook the transverse cable on cantilevers. U-brakes open automatically if you slam the wheel against them during removal (except on bikes with vertical dropouts).
2. If there's a peg on the inside of your right chainstay, lift the chain onto it with one finger.
3. Remove the wheel. For front flats, lift the bike by the handlebar with one hand while removing the wheel with the other. For rear flats, grip the saddle with one hand and lift. Remove the wheel with your free hand by pushing it forward (horizontal dropouts) or down (vertical dropouts). If you don't have a chain holder, shake the chain off the cog as you remove the wheel. If it resists, lift it with one finger.
4. Rest a mountain bike on its left side. Do the same with a road bike or, for rear flats, prop it on the front wheel and handlebar by turning the wheel so the brake caliper arm contacts the down tube. This may require pulling the shift lever back slightly.
5. Release any air still in the tire. With presta valves, unscrew the top and press it with one finger. With Schraders, press the hook on your tire lever into the valve.
6. To remove a tire by hand, pinch a section opposite the valve with your left (or weaker) hand. Let the wheel hang below (valve at bottom). Roll the tire back with your fingers so your left thumb is under the tire and your

fingers are on top. With your right hand, work around
the tire, pinching and wiggling its beads toward the central deep section of the rim. As you do this, exert upward
pressure with your left thumb. (See the illustration below.) This will create slack at the top of the tire. After

To remove the tire and tube together, pull upward with your left thumb
while pinching the beads into the central deep section of the rim with
your right hand.

working around the rim, grasp the tire with your right hand, adjacent to your left. Rest the bottom of the wheel on the ground and lift the tire and tube, rolling them over the edge of the rim with the heels of your hands.

To remove a tire with levers, insert one under a bead, opposite the valve stem. Push it down toward the spokes, using the rim edge as a fulcrum, thus prying a small section over the rim. Hold the lever in place against the spokes with one hand (or attach its hooked end to a spoke). Put another lever under the same bead about four inches from the first, and pry another section over the rim. Move four more inches, pry, and continue until the entire bead is removed. Then reach inside the tire, grasp the tube, and pull it out. To allow the valve stem to be removed, uncover it by pushing the tire away with the heel of your hand.

To assist inspection of the tire and rim, remove the other bead (it should come off easily). Otherwise, leave it in place.

7. Store the tube in your jersey pocket or seat pack so it can be patched later.

8. Run your rag around the inside of the tire in both directions while also inspecting the outside. If it doesn't snag, the tire is probably free of whatever caused the puncture. Otherwise, remove the offending object. If you touched the chain, clean your finger with the rag.

Installing a Tire

When mounting a tire, follow these steps.

1. Inflate your spare tube just enough to make it round. Place it inside the tire, inserting the valve stem first. (If one bead remains on the rim, place the valve in the rim hole and tuck in the tube. Skip steps 2 through 5.)

2. Lean the wheel against your shins, valve hole on top.

3. Hold the tire and tube combination (valve on top) with both hands, place a portion of the closest bead on the rim and insert the valve stem a quarter of the way into the rim hole. (If the stem doesn't fit through the

rim strip easily, enlarge the hole at home later with scissors.)

4. Work the bead onto the rim by moving your hands apart, away from the valve stem. If this is difficult, pull all of the tube out of the tire except the section near the valve stem.

5. Now that one bead is on the rim, tuck the tube into the tire and onto the rim, making the second bead flush against the outside of the rim. If the tube resists, let some air out, but don't deflate it completely.

6. Starting at the valve stem, work the bead onto the rim with both hands. Push the valve stem up into the tire so its thick base isn't trapped beneath the bead, then pull it down firmly.

   Use the heels of your hands to roll the bead onto the rim. It's usually difficult to complete the last section, but remember, it doesn't take strength, just good technique. Try releasing a little more air to create room inside the tire. If it still resists, use the removal pinch technique to move the beads to the central well of the rim. This should provide enough slack to pop the bead in place.

7. Partially inflate the tire and spin the wheel to see if the beads are seated. (This problem is rare with this installation technique.) The bead line molded in the tire's sidewalls should appear just above the rim on both sides.

8. Finish inflating the tire, return your pump to the frame, and store any tools you may have used.

9. Center the wheel in the frame by pulling it all the way into the dropouts. On rear wheels, place the freewheel inside the chain, just above the derailleur, with the chain engaged on the smallest cog. Close the brake quick-release or reattach the transverse cable.

10. If the chain came off the chainrings, hand pedal it back on.

Now get moving or you'll be late after all!

■ CREDITS

The information in this book is drawn from these and other articles in *Bicycling* magazine.

"An Editor Becomes a Commuter" Ed Pavelka, "Me, the Bike Commuter," May 1991.

"No Excuses, Only Solutions" John Kukoda, "You: The Bicycle Commuter?" April 1988.

"End Your Fear of Riding in Traffic" Scott Martin, "The Road Worrier," March 1990.

"Unwritten Traffic Codes" James Hargett, "Keeping Friendly Drivers Friendly," August 1989.

"Maneuvers for City Cycling" John Kukoda, "City Cycling," April 1986.

"Simple Steps for Avoiding Accidents" Bob Katz, "Ride Fast, Hog the Road, Act Like Traffic," July 1988

"Cycling Rules for Any Road" Sara J. Henry, "It's a Jungle Out There," March 1988.

"Rainy-Day Rides" Geoff Drake, "Rain Man," October/November 1989; John Kukoda, "Slick Street Survival," January 1986.

"How to Ride in Snow and Ice" John Kukoda, "Winter Cycling," December 1986.

"Safety at Dawn, Dusk, and in the Dark" John Kukoda, "Lighten Up," January/February 1989; Liz Fritz and Liz Smutko, "You, the Bike Commuter," May 1991; Jim Langley, "Take Back the Night," October/November 1989.

"Nutrition Guide for Everyday Riders" Virginia DeMoss, "Eater's Digest," March 1991.

"Best Breakfasts for Commuters" Virginia DeMoss, "Break Fast," April 1991.

"Cycling with a Cold" Dawn Welch, "The Cold War," January/February 1991.

"The Effects of Air Pollution" Edmund R. Burke, Ph.D., "Exhaust(ion)," August 1988.

"Converting Your Bike for Commuting" Ross Kerber, "Quick Conversions," May 1988.

"Basic Bike Care" Jim Langley, "Basic Bike Care," January/February 1989; Jim Langley, "Take a Bike Out of Crime," April 1990.

"Weatherproofing Your Bike" Jim Chapman, "Weatherproofing," December 1988.

"All-Weather Clothing" Geoff Drake, "Rain Man," October/November 1989; Liz Fritz and Liz Smutko, "You, the Bike Commuter," May 1991.

"Accessories That Make Commuting Convenient" Liz Fritz and Liz Smutko, "You, the Bike Commuter," May 1991.

"How to Fix a Flat in 5 Minutes" Jim Langley, "Five-Minute Tire Repair," June 1990.

Photographs

Mike Shaw: page 10; Carl Doney: page 24; Ed Landrock: page 37; Donna Chiarelli: pages 53, 101,103, 105; Michael Furman: pages 87, 88.

Illustrations

Sally Onopa: pages 25, 96, 97, 110.